A Bronx Memoir

Growing Up

In

Highbridge

1940s—1950s

By Lester Fritz
Highbridge Guy

Highbridge Guy

Growing Up In The Bronx

In The Bronx
1940s & 1950s

Fogarty, Pat, Ed.

Subtitle: Highbridge Guy.

Granite Publishing: December 2020:

ISBN

978-1-950105-23-6

HB1551065906

9 8 7 6 5 4 3 2

Print Edition

Printed in the United States of America

Granite Publishing

Prescott & Dover

About the Author

Lester Fritz was born, raised, & educated in the Highbridge section of the Bronx. As a career, Lester worked for 50+ years in different phases of the food industry. He and his lovely wife, Dotty, are now retired and enjoying life on the shores of the Chesapeake and Delaware Canal. Lester and Dotty have cruised the Chesapeake Bay for decades on their boat; *Little Kidd Too*. First with their children and now with their grandchildren A history buff, Lester lovingly wrote this book for his children and grandchildren to let them know what it was like coming of age in the middle of the last century.

Author's Note to the Reader

This book is like a time-capsule. Inside the cover you will find a collection of topics and personal reminiscences of life as it was, growing up in a great Bronx neighborhood in the 1940s and 50s. It's about a time when trolley cars and subway trains were the best way to travel in the Bronx. A place where a fruit peddler and his horse-drawn wagon were still a common sight. A time when parents would let their kids play outside on the Bronx sidewalks until the streetlights came on. It was an era when courtyard singers and musicians could earn a living by performing and collecting tips tossed from apartment windows. Etched into that period are the memories of World War II and the opportunity to observe the Greatest Generation from a front-row seat. Finally, it's a love story about meeting the girl you would marry and spend the rest of your life with.

—Lester Fritz—HIGHBRIDGE GUY

Highbridge Guy

Growing Up In The Bronx

In The 1940s & 1950s

Prologue

As I look back to the early years of my life, I can't help thinking about how different things are now from what they were during my childhood growing up in the Highbridge section of the Bronx. How our lives are lived in what seems to be "just a blink of the eye" never ceases to amaze me when I'm in one of my remembrance moods. Certainly, we would like to believe that we are living our lives in an interesting and meaningful time in history. I think my life has taken me through one of the greatest scientific periods in history. My father, on the other hand, firmly believed that he had lived through the Golden Age of sports.

I've often found myself thinking why didn't I ask my parents and grandparents more about how life was when they were growing up.

How things in their lives changed as they grew older. Once that opportunity to ask is gone and your parents, aunts, uncles, and grandparents are gone that opportunity to learn firsthand about your history can never come again.

I decided to begin this project as a way of letting my children and those that follow them know a little about how it was to grow up and come of age in the middle of the Twentieth Century. And, a little about the history of the family members who preceded them. Yes, it doesn't seem that long ago that time of which I speak. But on closer examination then and now are light years apart in the way we live, especially if comparing the inner city of my youth to the suburban upbringing of my children and grandchildren. Some of the things on which I dwell may seem a bit mundane, but it is the little things in life that lead to the big changes in our way of living.

The first chapter of this remembrance I've titled the Apartment House and I begin there because it was usually the center of our lives. Fiction writers and Hollywood directors are always prone to describe the buildings we lived in as tenements. While that particular description may be technically accurate, I have always viewed a tenement as something akin to houses you might see in movies such as The Godfather, Once Upon A Time In America or Somebody Up There Likes Me. In other words, gritty, drab, and depressing buildings with clothes drying on lines, strange ethnic cooking aromas, and an unending babble of sound in a variety of languages.

The apartment houses we lived in were only somewhat like that. They were, for the most part, clean, fairly well-kept places that were both safe and comfortable to live in. I hope you enjoy this narrative of a kinder, gentler time. And I hope, by reading these remembrances, all of you will come to love New York City as I do. If I appear to ramble on at times, please let me do so. I will, hopefully, eventually get to the point. And if I seem to spend an undue amount of time on trivial, minuscule subjects... please bear with me. These are probably the most important nuances I'm trying to import to you from my store of memories of growing up in the Bronx in the middle of the 20th Century.

The Apartment House

When my grown children and their children talk about "their house" they are picturing a single-family home of one or two floors on a quiet street in a nicely kept neighborhood. An attached garage, finished basement, swimming pool, or hot tub usually completes the picture as well as a lawn, garden, and some nice landscaping.

When you spoke of "my house" in the Bronx of the 1940s, you were talking about a five or six-story building that was home to about twenty-five or more families each living in their own one, two, or three-bedroom apartment. If your apartment house was on a quiet side street or avenue, you probably had several apartments on the ground floor as well as on the upper floors. If you were located in a neighborhood shopping district with bus or trolley cars going past as we were, you might have two stores or commercial businesses on the ground floor facing the street. Then there would probably only be just two or three apartments to the rear of the building on its ground floor.

Another popular apartment house configuration was a double building with a central courtyard entrance between them. For some reason, buildings of this style were frequently six floors high rather than five. If a building was five stories or less, it was most likely a "walk-up" (A descriptive term that has come into popular use now, but one that we rarely used back then), which meant it didn't have an elevator. If your family, or your best friend's family, lived on the top floor you would most likely develop some well-muscled legs and lung capacity

3

from trips up and down the stairs to your apartment or your friend's to see if he "could come out to play" or "go to the movies." If you were lucky enough to have an elevator in your building, you got to save on the legs and lungs a little.

Hallways and staircases were great places to hang out in with your friends, particularly in the cold weather months, to talk about the latest movies playing at the local theater (not "the Cineplex", nobody back then would have known what that meant) or which teachers gave too much homework or what sports team, movie actress or anything else you can think of was "the best." Hanging out in somebody's hallway was sort of like hanging out at the Mall today, but without the temptation to spend money or eat fast food (another term that had no meaning back then) It was also, probably, the first place you ever "made out" or got that first kiss you'd been dreaming about.

During the winter, when you were young enough to still be "sleigh riding" (sledding) or building snow forts and having snowball fights (or pelting passing trolleys or buses with snowballs), hallways were great places to warm hands, feet, and noses while waiting for your gloves, hats, and scarfs to dry on the radiator under the staircase by the building's mailboxes. The combination of wet, snow-encrusted wool on cast iron steam radiators gave off a sickening, obnoxious smell I can still remember after more than half a century. Of course, all the wool item shrunk with this drying method and had to be stretched like crazy to ever get them on your hands again.

During the warmer months of the year, the apartment house became part of some of our games. It was not unusual for a game of *Hide and Seek* or *Ring-O-Levio* to include such parameters as "any place we can see from here plus all the (apartment) houses on this side of the street and their roofs."

This meant you were free to hide or chase in any of a half dozen houses and their rooftops where you could go from one building to another as easily as you could by using the sidewalk downstairs.

One of the biggest problems apartment dwellers faced was finding parking for your car (if you were lucky enough or crazy enough to have a car in the city back in those days. My dad had a car and was lucky enough to rent a garage under a row of stores adjacent to our building. It cost him $11.00 a month to know he had a close parking site for his '49 Ford. (Our family's rent on our apartment was $42.00 for all the years we lived there. Thank God for New York City rent control. Along about the time that I started to drive, the city instituted alternate-side of the street parking. Signs would be posted indicating that you couldn't park on this side of the street on Mondays, Wednesdays, and Fridays. On the other side of the street were signs that told you No Parking on Tuesdays and Thursdays. This did not present a problem if you were fortunate enough to have an off-street garage. When I got married and moved to Sheridan Avenue, a little bit east of my former Highbridge neighborhood, I joined that group of city automobile owners who raced back from their downtown offices every evening to frantically move their cars to the other side of the street before all the spots were filled for the next day. Sort of automobile checkers or chess.

But, back to the apartment house. The following page shows a picture of mine, as it looked when we lived there. Our windows were the four right-hand ones on the second floor—the only ones without awnings

As you and your circle of friends got a little older, hallways remained a prime gathering place. The topics of discussion might still be basically the same, but added in now would be who likes who in the neighborhood, how

best to let someone you liked know it, what high schools you were trying to get accepted at, and who had a job lined up for the coming summer. By this stage in life, you got to pick the best apartment house hallway and you sent the snow-covered, freezing, snot-nosed kids to dry their snow-encrusted wool caps and gloves in a less desirable hallway in another building.

Since our house was located on a major bus and trolley route, a commercial business and shopping area developed and we had two stores in the front of our building with big plate glass windows and entrances open from the sidewalk. The two businesses sat on either side of the entrance door to our lobby and hallway. One was Herman's Dry Goods Store and the other (which was located directly beneath our apartment) was a cleaning establishment. While "dry goods" may not conjure images of Macy's or Kohl's or even K-Mart, Herman's was a one-room operation but did a heck of a business in our neighborhood.

As the name implies, "the cleaners" cleaned and pressed clothes for families in the neighborhood. It was a necessary business conveniently located right at a bus stop, so for families that lived a block or two away from the bus line a housewife could say to her husband, "Honey, make sure you stop at the cleaners when you get off the bus tonight and pick up your blue suit and my topcoat." The cleaners should not be confused with the "laundry", which mostly washed and pressed shirts and was almost always run by a Chinese family. The well-known phrase "No tickee, no shirt!" was the cultural forerunner of "Can I supersize that for you?" The laundry was universally called "the Chinese laundry" as if there might be another kind around.

The cleaners, on the other hand, was for dry cleaning or "Martinizing", a word that appeared on the front window of every dry cleaners in the city. They usually boasted of One Hour Martinizing, but I don't think anyone even knew what Martinizing was or ever seriously tried to get a suit dry cleaned and pressed in an hour.

The most impressive part of "the cleaners", which was the way we referred to this store, was a very large pressing machine that weighed probably a couple of hundred pounds. This cast iron, steam breathing monster looked like two heavily padded ironing boards. The top half would be raised by a manual lever and the cleaned and dampened articles of clothing would be laid out on the lower half. After the article was stretched out and fairly wrinkle-free, the top half would be lowered to press the clothing with a mighty blast of steam from holes located in both halves of the presser behind the padding. It might take several position changes and pressings to finish the article to the satisfaction of the operator and to get them to a fully dried state before being put on a hanger. A large cloud of steam shot out the back window of this establishment into the courtyard with every pressing and rose past the windows of our apartment immediately above it like Old Faithful erupting. I have absolutely no recollection of this being annoying or upsetting to us in any way. I would characterize it as being about the equivalent of the traffic noises we listened to out the *front* windows of our apartment. It was no big deal. It was the sound of home.

The family in the apartment next to us at the front of the building were located right above Herman's and led a peaceful and boring existence without the clouds of steam several times a minute. Herman's occupied a space that was roughly the size of a two or three-car garage and that counted his backroom storage area, lavatory, and changing room. He was as much a part of the life of our building as any of the families that lived there and he specialized in ladies' and children's clothing. Although he ran this business for many, many years, I have no idea where he lived except that it wasn't in our neighborhood. Herman's display windows were always in season, but I especially remember his unending assortment of kid's bulky snowsuits, mittens, and knitted hats. During the spring and summer months, ladies' summer smocks and sundresses for little girls would be displayed on hangers right out on the sidewalk.

In addition to these two stores that were located right in our building, you could, in less than two minutes, walk to a grocery store, meat market, produce store, two bakeries, 2 candy stores, a shoemaker, a liquor store, and a Jewish deli. All things considered, living in an apartment house on a side street may have been a little quieter and peaceful, but nothing could beat the convenience of living on the main commercial avenue with such a good mix of businesses like that, in addition to the trolley or bus stop being right outside the entrance to your house.

This photo of my brother, Jim, and some friends was taken on the day they made their First Holy Communion. They are standing on the front "stoop" of 1390 Ogden Avenue (notice the number on the glass panel of the front entrance doors) If you didn't already know what month is traditional for receiving this sacrament, you could guess it was May. The summer dresses hanging on the front of Herman's store indicate the approach of warmer weather and the sign in the cleaner's window advertising fur storage as an offered service indicates that colder weather is behind us in the neighborhood and an apartment had few and small closets. Incidentally, the Fritz kids were all blondes (so you know which one is my brother) Whenever the gang ran from some mischief or other, we always heard the complaint, "I don't know their names, but that blond kid was one of them"

At the very top of the hall-staircase was a steel door that led out onto the roof of the building. The roof consisted of thick tar and a parapet that I always remember as being pretty short (like two-foot-high or so—maybe 30 inches) and not very substantial considering you were five floors up. Openings in the parapet led to iron ladders that would let you descend to the fifth-floor fire escape and from there down steel stairs that would take you to the fire escapes on each of the lower floors. More about the roof, the cellar, and the courtyard will be told in future chapters of my story.

In addition to being the safety feature they were meant to be, fire escapes had several other popular uses. Foremost of these alternative uses would have to be Christmas tree storage. Although a family might buy its tree a week or ten days before Christmas, city dwellers almost always waited until Christmas eve to put it up and decorate it. It's interesting to mention that my cousin, Dave, and his folks sometimes had their trees up two to three weeks ahead of us like their other suburban neighbors, a sign of things to come as we eventually moved our families to the suburbs and the country. The largest cooking pot or bucket in the house would be filled with water and the tree (still all tied up with string... plastic tree netting had not yet been invented) would be stood in the pot and, possibly lashed to the railing of the fire escape until Christmas Eve. During particularly cold years, it might become necessary to melt solid ice to separate your tree from the pot on Christmas Eve.

Another popular use of a fire escape was as a place, to put couch cushions and pillows out on, to sleep on hot, sticky summer nights. I guess you could call it the 1940s &

1950s version of air conditioning, which in those days was only available in movie houses. Other uses would usually center around house parties. You might put the keg of beer out there in a tub of ice, or a musician, usually a fiddler or concertina player, or as a place for three or four overflow guests to gather. You could probably do any one of the above, but space would not allow more than one of those uses at a time.

Some tenants might use a fire escape as a place to get some sunlight and air for their household plants, but had to be careful not to overdo it or they might incur a warning from the building's super or even the neighborhood cop on his walking beat that they were creating an obstacle that could be dangerous in the event of a fire in the building. A fireman from the closest firehouse might also take notice of blockages on fire escapes as he checked the neighborhood's fire hydrants or alarm boxes. Now, that was community policing in the middle of the twentieth century.

On the following page, note the five-story apartment houses, fire escapes, and stores and businesses at sidewalk level. Every neighborhood had its own flavor and ethnic make-up but the ubiquitous apartment house could usually be found in every one of them. It was the heart of the neighborhood, the place to which families returned at the end of the work or school day and from which they would begin their new day tomorrow. More on the apartment house in later observations, but when you hear someone refer to them as "tenements", know that thousands of them were anything but tenements, being excellently built of brick and plaster over lathe with real

tile in the bathrooms, hardwood and parquet flooring being quite commonplace in the living rooms, dining rooms, and master bedrooms. Paneled or box molding was also the norm in all rooms. Many people of my generation realized later in life; "Hey, I guess we were poor, but we didn't know it!"

A typical New York City street scene in 1942. In the upper left corner of the picture note that the side of that apartment house is concave towards the back of the building. If another apartment house had been built next to it, a concave setback facing that one would have formed a courtyard or airshaft to allow light and air down to those rear windows.

Marble and granite were often included on the outside facing of apartment houses and even murals and frescos were frequently used liberally in the lobbies and entrance foyers of many of them. Gifted European immigrants had built them sturdy and beautiful between the 1890s and 1930s

Some more extravagant apartment houses boasted courtyard fountains, gardens, and benches for the residents to enjoy. The Noonan Plaza, a complex right across the street from my grammar school was a group of several apartment houses going around the block and facing outward on three streets. In the central courtyard ringed by these buildings, was a half-acre size pond surrounded by wrought iron fencing, shrubbery, and flowers. On the peaceful, glassy surface of the pond glided two enormous white swans. And on a little island in the center was a pretty impressive looking

lighthouse. It wasn't quite Park Avenue, but it didn't look like the rest of our Highbridge neighborhood either. If one of your classmates told you he lived in the Noonan Plaza (or Towers), you were impressed. Oh, and for little kids exploring the neighborhood and looking to get into some mischief, let me tell you .. those swans are nasty, especially when they're nesting. More on certain aspects of the Apartment House in future installments. Stay tuned.

The Superintendent

We called him the "Super" and he was the most important part of how your apartment house worked. He stoked the furnace so that the tenants could have hot water and steam heat. If you had a bad Super, you (and every other tenant in the building) would beat on the cast iron radiator with a cooking pot or some other metal instrument to let him know you were cold or that there was no hot water in the shower.

The Super would mop down the staircases, floor landings, hallway, and lobby one or more times each day. He would "pull" the dumbwaiters each evening after supper to collect the day's garbage and then transfer the trash to garbage cans in the basement. There were usually three or four dumb-waiter shafts in the average apartment house, situated so that two adjoining apartments on each floor could use the same shaft.

Marks on the rope pull let him know at what level in the shaft the dumbwaiter was and then he would ring a buzzer in each apartment on that floor to let the tenants know it was time to put their bags of trash on the dumbwaiter. If the dumbwaiter was already too full when you opened the access door, you would just yell down to tell him that and he would bring it all the way down to the basement, unload it, return it to your floor, and ring again. Actually, you would hear it moving back up the shaft and you knew it was for you so you would probably open your dumbwaiter door before he even had to ring the buzzer. This was also a good time to say hello to your neighbor across the shaft, just in case you hadn't seen each other in the hall or at the mailboxes in a couple of days. It was also important to remember to be dressed as you would if you were answering your apartment door as you would be looking right into each other's kitchens or foyers.

The superintendent had to carry quite a few metal garbage cans up to street level and out to the curb a couple of times each week for the city sanitation trucks to pick up. This was not a job for wimps. Then on a once a week or once every other week schedule, he had to carry up other cans filled with cinders and ashes from the furnace. These were heavier than the regular trash cans, so he did not actually carry them. He had a heavy-duty steel dolly and would pull one can at a time out of the basement, across the courtyard, and up about twelve or thirteen steps through a concrete tunnel up to the sidewalk level. It seems to me there were days during the coldest months that every apartment house on the block had out a dozen to two dozen cans of cinders at the curb.

The city sent trucks to pick up the cinders and then stored them in yards all over the five boroughs of New York until they were needed during snowstorms when they would be spread on snow-covered and icy streets. The spreading of salt and other melting chemicals was still years in the future. As the snow-covered streets dried out and the snow melted off, the cinders would simply be crushed into a fine sand by truck, car, and bus tires and would eventually find its way into the storm sewers.

The Super's wife, and kids as they got older, often took over the lighter jobs like "pulling trash" and mopping the stairs and halls. They oversaw the basement areas that were available to the tenants for storage of such things as baby carriages, bicycles, and tricycles and scheduled new deliveries of coal when it was needed.

In return for all these responsibilities, the family lived rent-free in their basement apartment to the rear of the building and may have had their utilities paid for, as well. I'm not sure about that. The Super also usually had a full time outside job to cover his other needs, maybe something in maintenance, mechanical or janitorial services, but maybe not.

Most apartment houses of the time had awnings made of canvas duck to be put up each year when the sunniest months approached. These would be put on each of the front windows of the building and were another task done by the Super. Also, of course, taking them down and storing them after the brighter, hotter months had passed.

A typical Bronx apartment house in the Summertime.

The super would post a notice in the foyer or hallway informing his tenants of the date he would be putting up or taking down the awnings, which were usually striped canvas duck. The framework or armature of the awning could be folded up if the shade wasn't needed in a room or area of the apartment at the time. The awnings were only rarely put up on the north-facing windows of a building. Note the amount of marble and granite used on even this very average building and the artistry of the friezes and coins used on and above the windows.

The superintendent would respond to tenants' calls for help with clogged drains, dripping faucets and pipes or radiators, and any electrical problems that might arise. Most building supers also took great pride in keeping the brass mailboxes located in the foyer, lobby, or somewhere in the ground floor hallway, polished and buffed until the tenants and the mailman could see themselves reflected in its polished surface.

During the winter months, he was responsible for shoveling the snow from the sidewalk in front of his building, not just a path, but the entire sidewalk from the base of the building to the curb and from one end of the building's front to the other.

In addition to all of these regular responsibilities, some supers acted as the "rental agents" for the apartment house owner, collecting the monthly rent from each tenant and showing vacant apartments to prospective newcomers. The smart apartment dweller tried to stay on the good side of his super. If an apartment was about to come open (vacated) you might have the word in with him to let you know as soon as he heard. You might be looking for an apartment with more bedrooms for a growing family or for a relative that was about to get married and needed their own place.

Need a baby sitter? An extra set of eyes to keep tabs on your mischievous kids. The super was your man… and he did it all for free <u>and</u> without even being asked. A good super would ride herd on any kids he caught hanging out in the halls. You could possibly hear, "I'm gonna let you kids hang out and warm up, but if I start to see candy wrappers and any other junk left around or if I get complaints from any tenants that you're too loud or using bad language or that they had a hard time getting around you kids to go up the stairs then you'll be out of here for good. Deal?" I'll bet that New York City superintendents did more to delay the eventual onslaught of spray paint graffiti than any other person, job title, or department in the city.

There were many other mischiefs we could get into, but sooner or later the super would catch us at that, too. Up on the roof, for example. "So you're the ones throwing the snowballs down on the people waiting for the bus across the street. I know most of you and if it happens again I'll be telling your parents. And I'll stop letting you sunbathe up here come next summer." Yeah, the super was a little bit of everything to a good apartment house.

Going to School in the Bronx 1940s & 1950s

If there was one thing a kid had to learn in the Bronx before going to school, it was how to walk. Sure, every kid learned how to walk by the time he or she was two years old and spent the next three years perfecting the technique by playing, running, climbing, and jumping on sidewalks, parks, and all kinds of playground equipment. All under the close supervision of mom.

But there came a time, legislated by the City of New York and/or the Archdiocese of New York when you were deemed old enough to attend grade school and become an educated little person. Your parents had the choice of sending you to a public school (in our case P.S. 11) or a Catholic elementary school (also in our case, Sacred Heart School) known in our parish community as Sacred Heart Highbridge. So on a late August or early September day, my mother "walked me" to Sacred Heart and back to our apartment house and would do so for the next several days until she was satisfied I had the route down pat. These were not the leisurely walks we previously took to the park but walks to get there by a certain time.

Unlike what my children and grandchildren would experience on their first days of school, there would not be a big yellow school bus waiting for us at the end of a driveway each morning. I can't even remember how old I was by the first time I saw a yellow school bus. No, our forte would be walking, not riding and we got it down pat right from the start. Very few of my classmates' parents owned a car, and if they did, there was a very good chance it was garaged quite a few blocks from where they lived to be used only on weekend trips.

On that first day of school, we emerged from our apartment houses (still in tow with mom as we would be for a few more days) with brand new Thom McCann shoes on, new knickers, knee socks, dress shirt, and clip-on tie. As the weather got colder, wetter, or snowier, we would add galoshes (heavy rubber boots with snaps) gloves, hats, and mackinaws or Navy peacoats to our list of necessary outerwear. Mackinaws were heavy woolen coats, usually in plaid with a zip-up hood. Peacoats looked exactly like the ones that U.S. Navy enlisted men were issued, even down to the two rows of plastic buttons with anchors embossed on each of them. Both coats were very warm for kids who would always be walking to school.

Classes at Sacred Heart were co-ed for the first four years and we soon fell into the routine of the school, which included morning classes and afternoon classes with a one-hour lunch break in between. There were no cafeteria or lunchroom facilities, so everyone got back into outdoor clothing around 11:30 and walked home for lunch. Stay-at-home-moms were the norm back then so lunch would be on the table or almost ready when we got there. Then it would be time to get dressed again and head out for what was for me, a five-block walk to the schoolyard for a few minutes of horseplay before the Nun rang her big brass hand-bell and we formed lines by the class we were in to return to our afternoon school work.

Upon entering fifth grade, the boys were moved to the other end of the school and the girls remained in all-girl classes on their side. We began or continued to form friendships that would last the rest of our lives.

This was the fifth grade class of 1946. I can still name most of them after more than seventy years because our class remained the same until we graduated four years later in 1950. I'm seated at the back of the 2nd row, Jack Fogarty is in the next row, (second from the back) and Gerry Lenaghan is in the last row against the wall (second from the back). Tommy Farrell would join us the following year and the "Highbridge Big Four" would be launched.

As the school years went by, it was surprising how much trouble we could get into during that one-hour lunch break and the round trip to our homes to eat and then meet up for the return trip to school. At last, we were eighth-graders and our year focused on taking entrance exams to the different Catholic high schools in the city. I went to Rice, run by the Irish Christian Brothers, Gerry and Tom went to Cardinal Hayes and Jack went to All Hallows.

When I first started at Rice, I would take the Ogden Avenue bus down to 161st, which was the site of Yankee Stadium, where I would then take the IRT subway to the 125th Street station then walk crosstown from Lexington Avenue to Lenox Avenue and the school. That trip would cost me $.30 a day, fifteen cents for the bus and fifteen cents for the subway. Then, someone pointed out to me that if I walked down the Highbridge steps and took the New York Central commuter train to 125th Street from the Highbridge station, it was only an eleven cent fare and most of the time the conductor didn't even get to you by 125th Street. So it was a free trip with a nicer class of commuters. I must admit that we became very expert in avoiding the conductor on this twelve-minute trip.

During the four years I attended Rice, our swimming team remained the most powerful of any high school in the city. That run began with our freshman team in the 1950 – 1951 season and continued right through our next three years of varsity competition. It probably didn't hurt that we had a swimming pool in the basement and could practice daily before and after our classes. Pools were virtually non-existent in other schools in the city in those days and our opponent teams had to struggle to get practice time at city pools, hotel, and club pools whenever and wherever they could. The Irish Christian Brothers had purchased a former YWCA building in which to establish Rice High School and that's the only reason we wound up having our own pool to practice in.

Completing my Catholic education with four years at Iona, another Irish Christian Brothers school, I had run the full gamut of walking, running, commuting by city transit, hitchhiking, and driving a car I inherited from my father.

Sacred Heart Grammar School Highbridge
Built in 1926, still in use today.

Getting Around By Trolly, Bus, & Subway

City kids faced a great adventure when they could finally convince their parents that they knew some part of the transportation system well enough to go someplace on their own without fear of getting lost. For the princely price of a nickel, you could get on a trolley car and with unlimited free transfers travel anywhere in the Bronx or upper Manhattan. For more exotic and adventurous destinations like lower Manhattan's theater district (Times Square), Central Park and museums, or Brooklyn's Rockaway Beach or Coney Island, the subway was a better mode of travel because of the distances involved.

Of course, youngsters had to gradually win their parents' confidence that they knew how to get where they wanted to go and, since there is always strength and safety in numbers, it helped if several friends were going with you. Early travel adventures would most likely be a trip from our neighborhood, the Highbridge section of the Bronx, across the bridge to the Washington Heights neighborhood of upper Manhattan. That trip would take all of ten minutes with about five stops, but when we climbed down off that trolley or bus there were three movie theaters to choose from just two blocks from each other instead of just the one movie house in our neighborhood. Also, that Washington Heights section was a major uptown shopping center with a Department store, Wertheimers, clothing and shoe stores, and a really big Woolworth's 5 and 10 cent store.

Taking the same trolley line in the opposite direction would bring you right outside the left-field façade of Yankee Stadium in about fifteen minutes. That was a ride of ten blocks and was also the end of the line for that route, but if you had asked for a transfer when you got on you could continue your trip on one of several lines that met just outside the stadium.

Trolleys ran on major routes everywhere in the city and most riders could walk home in no more than two or three blocks after getting off at their stop. They were so ubiquitous, convenient, and reliable that untold numbers of New Yorkers never even bothered to get a driver's license when they came of age or for much of their lives.

Trolley cars ran on steel rails embedded in streets that were paved with what we usually referred to as "cobblestones". In fact, the correct name of the cobblestones was Belgian blocks and they were quite similar to the product known today as landscape paving blocks, the E.P. Henry brand being one of the most popular in use today. The blocks had come to this country by the hundreds of tons as ballast in the holds of sailing ships.

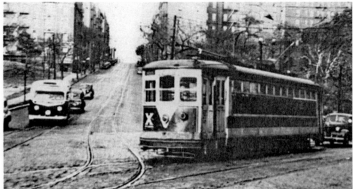

The photo shows a New York City trolley on Jerome Avenue in the Bronx in the late 1940s. If the photographer turned around and looked over his right shoulder, Yankee Stadium would be seen about three blocks away across open parkland and public baseball fields. The bus has just come down the Ogden Avenue hill from my Highbridge neighborhood. It heralds the approaching demise of the trolley as the major method of city transportation. Within the short span of just a few years, one route at a time, the trolley car would be completely replaced by the bus. I've always felt more effort should have been put into modernizing the trolley system rather than dismantling it.

The trolley ran on electricity supplied by a live line suspended by poles all along the routes they traveled. A spring-loaded armature on the trolley roof extended a contact rod to the live electric line above and was located at the rear of the car. The motorman stood at the center of the front of the car (but he did have a little swing out stool), not unlike the helmsman on a ship's bridge. When he reached the end of the line, he would move to the rear of the trolley to the other control station. Now that became the front of the trolley car. While waiting to begin his journey in the opposite direction, he would lower and tie down the armature that had been following the trolley and supplying its power. Then he would untie and extend the contact armature on what now became the rear of the trolley. One final adjustment, walking up the aisle and yanking all the seatbacks in the opposite direction so passengers would be facing front and he was ready to travel his route in the other direction. Passengers were allowed to move the seatbacks as well, which was very nice for a group of three or four to face each other.

Two double seats ran down each side of the center aisle and the seats and the seatbacks were caned. Hanging from the ceiling on each side of the aisle was a series of straps or porcelain handles for standing passengers to hold on to when underway. This gave rise to the slang expression "strap-hanger" to describe a regular bus, trolley, or subway commuter. Another term that came about from this form of transportation was the name of the baseball team we know today as the Dodgers. They were originally known to their stalwart fans as the Trolley Dodgers, a reference to the pedestrians who regularly jay-walked and dodged the trolleys on busy Brooklyn streets on their way to the ballpark known as Ebbets Field. Despite the deep-seated history of the name to the borough of Brooklyn, it became just the Dodgers long before they left and took the name with them when they relocated to Los Angeles in 1957.

When trolley cars were the primary transportation, New Yorkers were yet to learn about noise pollution or air pollution. Sure, there was an ever-growing number of trucks, automobiles, and taxis in the city, but the worst offender to air and noise pollution would be the buses with their big, powerful engines when they finally replaced the trolley cars.

On the contrary, trolleys had no fossil fuel engines to choke pedestrians with and they passed almost silently with a rush of air and a shower of sparks occasionally shooting out like quiet fireworks from where the armature met the electric overhead wire. The loudest thing on a trolley, other than the very quiet clacking of the steel wheels as they crossed the expansion joints in the rails, was the bell used by the motorman to warn pedestrians and motorists of his approach.

When the cold of winter finally arrived, the University Avenue trolley would display a red ball from the armature wire to let everybody know that the lake at Van Cortland Park was frozen thick enough for ice skating. It was a nice gesture on the part of the New York City Transit Authority and it didn't hurt ridership any on a winter's evening when skaters in wool hats and scarves crowded in to ride the trolley to its northern terminus adjacent to the park's frozen lake.

That same trolley in the summertime would take us to Van Cortland to rent rowboats by the hour to get out on the lake, which was the closest thing to living out in the country to a city kid. Other lines would carry us across the width of the Bronx to places like the Bronx Zoo, the Botanical Gardens, the beaches on the Bronx side of Long Island Sound, or to City Island to fish and crab from a dock or rented rowboat.

As we grew a little older, we got better at the transportation game as we went to high schools, colleges, and jobs downtown on a regular daily basis. The New York Central Railroad which had a station in Highbridge down a long flight of steps near the Harlem River became another option to getting around. When I went to Rice High School in Manhattan, I started freshman year by catching the Jerome Avenue train at 170th Street or 161st Street by Yankee Stadium. The subway token I used at the turnstile cost 15 cents. As I was getting ready to start sophomore year, some good soul informed me that if you went down those steps to the Central and caught the next train to Grand Central Terminal, I could make it to the 125th Street station in only fourteen minutes and the fare was 11 cents. But the real icing on the cake was that you paid your fare to the conductor on the train and if you could move forward or rearward to avoid him for 14 minutes, you made the trip for free. I must admit to some occasional guilt for all of the eleven cent fares I cost the NYCRR... but I usually get over it pretty quickly by chalking it up to becoming a "street smart" Bronx guy.

Until I was about 10 years old, the trolley and bus were really only the most efficient and practical mode of transportation there was. World War II put all former automobile manufacturers on a "war footing" turning out tanks, trucks, jeeps, and all sorts of other things essential to winning the war. Were you, fortunately, already the owner of an automobile, you were severely hampered in using it because of gas rationing and the shortage of necessary replacement parts and tires. So the trolley remained the public transportation mainstay until after VJ Day, which was Victory over Japan, by the way. The true Age of the Automobile arrived as auto manufacturers re-tooled to the first new models in four years, starting the real American love affair with their cars. Shortly thereafter, busses started replacing streetcars (trolleys) and, of course, the old reliable subway trains kept screeching along in their dark underground tunnels and on their elevated lines in the outer boroughs of Brooklyn, Queens, and my beloved Bronx.

Street Games We Played

Young city kids started interacting with their friends, schoolmates, and other kids "on the block" or in the neighborhood with role-playing games like war, cowboys and Indians, and cops and robbers. "Shoot 'em up" games like these did not lend themselves well to being played on the streets, sidewalks, or in the hallways or courtyards of our apartment houses.

To get the maximum benefit and the open space feel of the battlefield or the prairie or Western town, these games might be played in the local park, of which there was anywhere from one to several in any given neighborhood.

The parks were actually not the best setting for these games, however, since they were basically flat, open, mowed lawns surrounded by park benches that were, for the most part, occupied by older ladies talking, reading, or knitting or by younger ladies with strollers, baby carriages and even younger kids than we were... and who would usually cry a lot when we wouldn't let them join our game.

No, the best place for our cowboy and war games was "the lot" or the woods. It's important to understand the context of the lot in relation to living and playing in an urban setting. A lot was a piece of neighborhood ground that had not been built on or paved for parking. Chances are, it had some kind of huge rock outcropping or canyon-like hole that would make it too costly to level or dig a foundation in. It might have a couple of billboards on it, which was one way an owner could get some sort of value out of it. Unlike the park, the lot was not mowed or cared for in any way. Anything that grew in a lot was free to grow as tall as nature allowed, making good prairie land to crawl through. Rocks, boulders, and billboard frameworks made great high ground to defend in war games.

The problems with lots were several, foremost among them were that people in the neighborhood would walk their dogs there. And in those days nobody was walking their dogs with a bag to clean up after them. Concrete rubble, gravel, furnace cinders, or other excess building materials were sometimes dumped in neighborhood lots. Thankfully, almost everybody would refrain from dumping real garbage or refuse in a lot… at least, not back in the 1940s. Superintendents from nearby apartment houses might spread a can or two of furnace cinders at times if they had filled all their trash cans before the city collection for the week.

A great deal of broken glass found its way to lots. Glass was the chief container for almost any drink or beverage you could think of from soda to milk to beer and even though there was a deposit charged on most bottles and a refund available on their return, many still found themselves thrown against the rocks in local lots. The aluminum can was still way in the future.

Well, I guess you get the picture of playing in the lots. We ran and crawled through them, we fought and rolled around on the ground and the weeds in them, we got cuts from the broken glass and splinters from climbing the supporting framework of the billboards. There would be occasional falls from the billboards, frequently involving a broken bone or two. For a change of pace, we would go play in the "woods", which were pretty much lots with trees on them. Since they were usually a little more off the beaten trail, the woods had less doggy waste and less broken glass, but now we faced the hazards of briars, thorns, and poison ivy or sumac.

As we got a little older, our focus moved from the lots and woods to the streets and sidewalks with a variety of games and activities. Hide and Seek should be obvious to all. The catch to playing neighborhood hide and seek was in establishing the dimensions of the playing area. (i.e. – "All the houses on this side of the street from the basements to the halls and staircases with roofs included, etc.")

Ring-O-Leeveo was another big favorite, played much like Hide and Seek, but as the guy who was "It" caught other players, they were in jail near home base and someone who had not been caught yet could free them all if he could beat the "It" person to the home plate and shout "Ring-O-Leaveo." When you were "It", you would be the subject of great criticism and derision if you were a "homer" who wouldn't allow yourself to get too far from the base in your search for other players to capture. In the NHL or World Cup soccer, defense might be admirable. Not so much in Ring-O-Leevio or Hide and Seek.

35

Both of the above games had an element of danger involved in that kids running at high speed up and down sidewalks and across streets (and not always paying attention to anything but the game) could run into slower, older people with disastrous results or cut across vehicular traffic with even more disastrous results (screeching of brakes, angry shouts from motorists who were sure they were about to hit a kid, etc.)

When you became bored with these games of exertion, it was often-time for the most popular of all street games… Scully… some called it Skelzies.

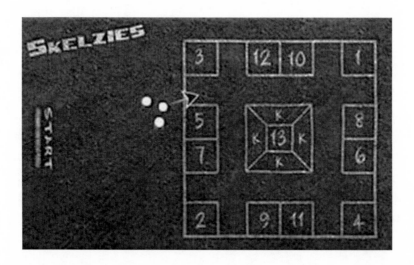

This is the diagram for Scully, well known to every kid who ever grew up in the city. It was drawn on the street in chalk. Never on the sidewalk. Most sidewalks were made of poured concrete and had a rather rough surface, which did not lend itself well to shooting a bottle cap across it by flicking it with your finger. The Scully map was drawn out in the middle of a blacktop tar street, which was relatively smooth and allowed for long accurate shots. A lightly traveled side street was best but you would still have to get up and move every time a car approached.

All that you needed to play Scully (nobody ever knew where the name originated) was a smooth surface, a piece of chalk, and a soda bottle cap for each player. Customizing your bottle cap was acceptable, so some of the more competitive kids would melt an old lead soldier to fill their bottle cap to make it heavier, smoother, and more accurate to shoot. Beginning at a point about eight to ten feet from Box #1, you shot in turn until your cap was in the #1 box and not touching any lines…. Then it was back and forth across the playing field until you got to Box #12. The final box, #13, was in the middle of the Dead Zone and had to be approached along one of the four diagonals. If you lost contact with that line, you were dead and out of the game. The same rule applied if you landed in the dead zone at any time while shooting back and forth from number to number.

Your opponents' bottle caps were fair game at all times and could be propelled many feet up or down the street with a really strong hit. Those players had to shoot themselves back to the playing field from wherever they had landed. A player who safely reached Box #13 became a "killer" and he permanently eliminated any player he hit from that point on.

A heated game of Scully taking place on a quiet side street of the neighborhood. This appears to be a game of players quite a bit younger than I remember playing in my day. Maybe the older kid leaning on the trunk of that car is teaching some of the younger neighborhood kids how to play the game.

As we approached the upper grades of grammar school and entered our high school years, games involving a ball would become our major activity.

There was little or no Little League baseball in the Bronx of the 1940s and '50s and Pop Warner or Little All-America football wasn't available in most of our neighborhoods either. These were almost exclusively suburban and country pastimes. Baseball fields were around but were usually only for the use of American Legion, high school, or beer league teams of young and middle-aged adults. As a neighborhood activity for us kids, baseball might best be described as going to a large open lawn area and having one guy hit fly balls that the rest of the gang could shag. Rooting for your favorite big league team and your favorite players was one thing; playing any form of organized baseball incorporating all the rules, etc. was quite another. There were several well-kept baseball fields just at the lower edge of our Highbridge neighborhood and ball games that were a little more organized were played there. The Fields, often called Diamonds, were just outside the famous and beloved Yankee Stadium.

The undisputed King of all NYC play equipment was a high-bounce Spaldeen

Most of the ball we played involved a smooth pink rubber ball that we called a Spaldeen, which was just slightly smaller than a baseball. When hit with a sawed-off broomstick, a Spaldeen (Spalding) could travel a full city block or more. The fielders would be spaced out for an entire block and when one of them made the agreed-upon number of catches, he became the batter. As you might guess, this game was called stickball. A stickball game could be ended at any time because the ball went down a sewer. If the group of players could come up with fifteen or twenty cents between them, they could purchase a new ball at the candy store which was usually just a few steps away from where we were playing. In the Bronx during the middle of the century, a candy store was only a few steps away from any place.

If we couldn't come up with the dough, there was always "Plan B". We'd remove the manhole cover from the top of the sewer and get one of the players to "volunteer" to be lowered and pulled back up after a thorough search. If we were really lucky, we might find and recover more than one Spaldeen if some previous players hadn't been able to get the manhole cover off. They probably weighed 75 or 80 pounds and removal had to begin with just fingertip strength.

When the Department of Sanitation was conducting inspections and cleanings, they used a five-foot-long steel bar with a slight bend at the end to lift the edge of a manhole cover. We tried to mimic that using our stickball bats but learned early on that we just broke the bat or completely chewed up the end so we would get splinters when we tried to bat with it afterward.

The ubiquitous city manhole cover. Access holes at the edges were to accommodate the pry bar the city workers used to lift an edge. But it could also be lifted by fingertips alone by a really big, strong kid. The cover pictured has N.Y.C. Sewer stamped on it, but many had Made In China or Made in India emblazoned on them.

Stickball was a very difficult game to play and I was never really good at it. The Spaldeen was not solid like a baseball but had compressed air in it. The ball was pitched like a baseball or on one bounce to the batter and if he really got a hold of it, it could be hit as high as the fourth or fifth floor of the apartment houses along the street and possibly come off the front façade of a building on an angle rather than just being hit down the center of the street.

Stickball, the hardest of New York City games with a ball. In this photo we see the great New York Giants center fielder, Willie Mays, loading up for a long one. Mays would sometimes skip pre-game batting practice at the Polo Grounds and warm up by playing a little stickball before a game.

Just as stickball was a form of baseball played in a city street, so was punch ball which didn't require the broom handle and could be enjoyed by players who were not that adept at stickball.

Punch ball was played at the intersection of two streets (hopefully quiet and less subject to vehicular traffic) that met at a 90-degree angle. The four corners of the curbs became home plate and the bases. The pitcher stood at the very center of the intersection and delivered the pitch on one bounce to the "batter" who punched the ball into play with his fist, fingers folded as flat as possible to the palm of the hand. There were no bats or gloves needed and a tennis ball was an acceptable substitute if a Spaldeen was not around. When the batter hit the ball, he ran the bases (corners of the intersection) and the next "batter" tried to hit him home. Scoring was involved, but unlike stickball, the rules of play pretty much followed the game of baseball.

There were many other varieties of ball to accommodate the playing skills and abilities of all ages. Captain Ball was played with any number of players against the wall of a building with each player defending his own concrete square of the sidewalk. The captain had the first square on the left end of the line and served the ball down the line by hitting it with the palm of his hand to take one bounce on the sidewalk and one against the wall. Whichever sidewalk square it landed in, that player could respond by slapping it the same way—back toward the captain or further to the right. When you missed you got a point and went to the last square on the right and everyone moved up one square. When the captain missed, he went to the last square but didn't get a point against him. Everyone moved up one square and the new captain became the server.

Another popular ball game was stoopball. Besides a ball, this game required a front stoop on an apartment house that had a 45-degree angle as part of its entrance decoration. The "batter" would throw the ball so that it struck the angle or the sharp edge below the angle to create a fly ball or a grounder (first bounce had to be in the street; not on the sidewalk) Each bounce was another base even though there was no actual base running involved. When the defensive players out in the street or on the opposite sidewalk caught a bell before it bounced in the street, that would be one out.

Girls played a variety of games such as hop-scotch, box ball, jacks, and any number of variations of jump rope. Few would consider these as "guy" games. However, most guys would probably try jumping rope at one time or another during their growing years. They frequently wound up looking very foolish, sometimes while lying on the sidewalk with the girls laughing at them. You could think of it as good preparation for later in life.

Handball courts were built in some of the larger parks in the late 40s and the 1950s. These courts became mainstays of mid-teenagers and young adults for getting some exercise. Johnny Ride a Pony, Mother May I, Follow the Leader and so many more crazy games with even crazier names proliferated through our growing years and all we really needed to play were a couple of other kids who were ready and willing and not being called to come up for dinner.

The Greatest Generation & Those before Them

My father and mother came into this world in 1910 and 1913 respectively and so are part of the Greatest Generation. They grew up in the midst of World War I. They lived through the pandemic of the Spanish Flu and other life-threatening diseases and illnesses that are, thankfully, no longer with us today.

Mom was Catherine Winifred Smith, the daughter of David Smith and Margaret Higgins Harrison. Dad was Lester John Fritz, son of Henry Richard Fritz and Margaret Connelly.

My parents entered their teens and became young adults at the height of the Roaring Twenties. Mom was always proud and happy to say she had been a flapper. A flapper was a rebellious young lady who bobbed her hair, wore short dresses to show off the lipstick on her knees (and, of course, on her lips and cheeks) and loved to party all night and dance the Charleston and the Lindy, which were all the rages at the time. Dad may have been a little more circumspect, but I'm not really that sure. He could be the life of any party by the time I came along, but I think mom's influence had a lot to do with that initially.

At the end of that era came a very rude awakening with the beginning of the Great Depression of 1929. My father graduated P.S. 11 in Highbridge, never went beyond that with his education. Instead, he entered the family business of sign hanging, something my grandmother had started to augment the FDNY salary of my grandfather. Dad, along with his brothers Harry and Willie, put up signs above storefront businesses all over the city, but mostly in the Bronx. The '20s were roaring, business was booming and everyone wanted to become an entrepreneur. The three brothers, along with sisters Ethel and Evelyn still lived in the family home at 1319 Sedgwick Avenue at the corner of Depot Place in Highbridge.

My mother came from a family of five children. James, John, Mae, Margaret, and herself. I believe they originally lived in lower Manhattan, but at some point, they moved uptown to Harlem around 135th Street. When my grandfather lost his wife in 1918, it was necessary to have the younger children cared for by relatives so he could continue to work as a tile layer. Jim and Mae were old enough to stay with Pop. Margaret, an infant, was sent to be raised by an aunt and John went with another aunt and uncle, the Dugans, who worked as housekeepers, gardeners, and horse handlers on a huge private estate in Peapack-Gladstone, New Jersey. Mom turned five years old that year. She was ready to start school so she stayed at home with her father, who hired a housekeeper to supervise her after-school activities. How does a tile layer hire a full-time housekeeper/Nanny? Pop wasn't "just a tile layer." He was an artist who took part in the building of swimming pools for some of the biggest and most famous resorts, hotels, and private residences in the nation. Working in all parts of the country when called upon, Dave Smith only tiled the top two feet and combing edge designs of those pools and was never short of work because of his reputation and artistry in the industry.

In her earliest school years, mom got to spend three complete summers with her brother at the big Peapack estate, which today is the official home of the U.S. Olympic Equestrian Team. Some of her happiest memories of growing up were about those summers spent at that estate where she rode and tendered horses, helped pick flowers for the mansion, and always watched with astonishment as her aunt pressed the letter B (the family initial) into individual home-made butter patties. It's nice to be rich.

The Smith family made a final move to Highbridge, where they lived on Woodycrest Avenue and where both Mae and mom would meet their future husbands. I'm not sure where mom's formal education stopped, but I think it was definitely more than my father, maybe even a high school diploma.

Dad was eighteen in 1928 when his father died. "Big Henry" Fritz was a horse handler and fireman and drove a three-horse team that pulled a ladder truck for H&L Co. 28 - FDNY. Shortly following his death, Uncle Harry's health began to fail, Uncle Willie joined the fire department and the sign hanging company came to a sudden end with the beginning of the Great Depression. Dad got a job as a contract painter specializing in high work, most of it consisting of painting the huge gas storage tanks that rose and fell in their steel frameworks all over the city. Sometime around 1932, Dad signed on to paint the George Washington Bridge. He lasted one full day but had a story he could tell for the rest of his life. "The height didn't bother me at all", he said," but the slightest. breeze that rippled the surface of the Hudson River below gave me, gave me tremendous dizziness"

Mom and Dad finally met in the early '30s and had a reasonably long courtship, marrying in 1933 and moving into a wood frame three-story apartment house on Sedgwick Avenue, almost across the street from the 44th Precinct – NYPD. I was born in1936 and came home to that apartment just a few doors down from my grandmother's home. With aunts and uncles to spoil me rotten just a few doors up the street, I enjoyed happy pre-school years. Mom would sometimes take me downtown to Tosca's Italian Restaurant on Wall Street, where she had worked for a few years as a waitress in a place dearly beloved by the stockbrokers, city hall workers, and newspaper people who worked nearby. Other times, I went with my grandma to a south Bronx firehouse where she had been given a job as an FDNY matron after my grandfather's death. She cleaned, made beds, and washed windows, while I was often entertained with the firemen and their equipment in between the exciting call-outs.

Eventually, we moved up the hill to Ogden Avenue, I started school at Sacred Heart and with the beginning of World War II, my father went to work in the Consolidated Shipyard on the Harlem River near Sedgwick Avenue and Fordham Road. The shipyard built and launched ocean-going tugboats; big, powerful boats that were strong enough to tow battle-scarred and battered cruisers and aircraft carriers back from battle areas to repair yards such as Pearl Harbor, Mare Island, Brooklyn Navy Yard, and Portsmouth, Virginia. The shipyard also had contracts to build sub chasers (PC's) which were somewhat like small destroyers (170 ft. long) and armed with depth charges and another armament. It was exciting for a young grammar school kid to attend the Saturday and Sunday launchings of these ships, and I attended quite a few and watched them slide down the ways and float out into the Harlem River with music blaring and flags cracking briskly in the breeze. From the year before the war started until the end of December 1945, the shipyard launched just about 50 of the sub chasers and almost the same number of the ocean-going tug boats. The tugs were all named to honor Native American tribes, such as the USS Cherokee, USS Kiowa, USS Seminole, etc.

My father became the youngest foreman in the yard, which employed 3,000 men and ran the blast furnace shop, where they heated and shaped the steel ribs and plates for the boats. He is pictured in the above photo in the back row fifth to the left of the center flag pole. As the war wound down, he had to begin laying off his crew and eventually was laid off himself. He worked the rest of his life in the construction industry as a wire lather and died at 63, after many years of fighting tuberculosis and emphysema from all the years he worked around and under asbestos on jobs.

My mother went back into the workforce around 1957, when dad became too weak to work. She was employed for 20 years or more with the Metropolitan Life Insurance Company and died in 1993 at the age of 80.

My parents and other relatives all loved the Highbridge neighborhood we lived in and so it wasn't very hard for me and my siblings to develop that love, as well. My sister, Barbara, was born in 1941, and my brothers, Jim and Russell in 1944 and 1952. We were the children of the Greatest Generation, as it came to be known, and we got to see, firsthand, what they did that earned them that title and great love by our nation.

Shopping in the Neighborhood

Later, when I grew to be a teenager, I would come to realize that every other Bronx neighborhood (probably every neighborhood in New York City) was a clone of my Highbridge neighborhood as far as stores went.

The kinds of stores we shopped in on Ogden Avenue were individually owned businesses run by people who were specialists in the kinds of products they sold. The same kinds of stores we had were duplicated in every other Bronx enclave... sometimes better run with better quality items for sale and sometimes not as good.

When my grown children need to do some food shopping today, they hop in their SUV, drive ten or fifteen minutes and spend another ten minutes walking across the parking lot and through the store to find the department, aisle, and, eventually, the items they are looking for. My mother gave me fifty cents and told me to run across to the Empire – "Look both ways crossing the street" – and get a loaf of Wonder Bread and a jar of peanut butter. When I went down the hall staircase, two at a time, ran through the hall, out the front door, and directly across the street, I was in the food store and at the register with my two items in three minutes. I was back in the kitchen with my mom spreading Skippy on my sandwich just five minutes after she sent me... with two cents change. "You can have the change. Get a Tootsie Roll or some Double Bubble gum after school."

The Empire Food Store was the place to food shop in our part of Highbridge. The shelves were low enough to see across the top of them clear to the other side of the store, all of about 40 feet with about four shopping aisles and two check-out registers. In size, it wasn't much different from the convenience stores of today. There was no produce department, the fruit and vegetable market was right next door to the Empire Market. The next store after that was a fresh meat market, so there wasn't much meat at the Empire either. Frozen food items were just coming into being as World War II was ending so, not much space was needed there, either. A beautiful, decorated cash register did nothing more than hold the bills and assorted change for transactions.

There were no tabulated register receipts. The clerk or owner added each of your items in grease pencil on the bag with the total before he packed it. You were free to check his math if you disagreed, but he was seldom wrong.

The Empire delivered your grocery order to your apartment if you chose, at no extra charge. However, it was expected you would tip the delivery boy when he delivered your order. This was often the first job a teenage boy would have. More on that later in "Jobs We Worked Growing Up"

Getting back to the Fruit and Vegetable store, it was family-run and named Morris', for the man who owned and ran it with a couple of brothers. One of the brothers would make a pre-dawn run to the Bronx Terminal

Markets each day to see what was being delivered that day by truck or rail. Their aim was to buy no more than that day's necessary supply or perhaps two day's worth. Miscalculations would mean a loss due to too much stock. In like manner, if the fruits or vegetables weren't fresh and presentable… more losses ensued.

This was almost the only store in the neighborhood whose owners felt they had a God-given right to the sidewalk in front of their store. So, every morning when they opened, they wheeled out boxes and boxes of vegetables and fruits, which they would stack as far out onto the sidewalk as they could get away with. Once in a while, the cop on the beat (foot patrol) would rap his nightstick on the cases furthest from the storefront and tell them they had to open the sidewalk more, that they were impeding pedestrian traffic.

This photo gives you the essence and feel of our neighborhood vegetable market in Highbridge. Inside the store, produce lined both sidewalls of the store with a central aisle down the middle. All the items outside would be wheeled inside on a handcart at closing time and left in the center aisle until the store reopened the following morning.

There was little or no refrigeration in the store. That was another prime reason that close attention had to be paid to the morning purchases at the main market. Seventy or seventy-five years later, I still remember the day

Sal or one of his brothers was carrying a stalk of bananas on his shoulder from their truck to the store and a really strange looking snake dropped out of the bunches of bananas. Tony ran out of the meat market with a meat cleaver and finished it off, but to this day I can't pick up a hand of bananas without looking really close to see if there are any snakes underneath.

Next door to Sal's fruit and vegetable market was Tony's Meat Market. This was also referred to as "the butchers" by the neighborhood residents and it had a meat case that ran the length of the store with Tony and his assistants behind the case and the customers in front of it. The butchers had a large, walk-in refrigerator/freezer at the back of the store and whenever they went in and out of the cooler you would get a glimpse of whole sides of beef or whole pig or lamb carcasses hanging on meat hooks. Boxed and pre-packaged meat was yet to come.

You want ground beef? Your neighborhood butcher would put any cut you want through a hand meat grinder until you said, "That looks about enough thanks."

The display case held trays of ice with the cuts of meat laying out for the customers to choose from. If you had a

special cut in mind, the butcher would cut and trim it to your specifications right in front of you on a huge meat cutting block. This would sometimes entail carrying out a whole side of meat on the shoulder from the cooler at the back of the market. Butchers wore white apron coats that were usually liberally smeared with blood from their wares, making several changes necessary as the workday wore on. If it was a hot day, the ice in the display cases would start to melt and leak out on the floor. The butcher had raised wooden decking on his side of the cases, but when the floors got wet and slippery on the customers' side they would spread sawdust on the floor for the safety of the customer.

These were the major food stores of our neighborhood, but there were many other stores of interest on our block. The candy store, drug store, bakery, delicatessen. Shoemaker and Chinese laundry will be addressed along with the neighborhood bar in another section. Each one was a unique and vital part of the neighborhood. Each with its own very special smells and memories.

Eventually, neighborhoods started to see the arrival of the grocery chain store. The Great Atlantic and Pacific Tea Company, (the A&P), Safeway, Grand Union, Gristede's, IGA, and many other national and local chains. They moved into storefronts on the main shopping streets that were not a whole lot bigger than the Mom and Pop corner grocery stores that they intended to compete with as one-stop shopping sites. And, the little local markets held their ground against those chain stores quite well. It would be quite a while before the really giant box stores and shopper's club that we know today would really put an impact on local neighborhood shopping. Perhaps, they still haven't in the neighborhoods of the inner city. It would be nice to think those neighborhood "Mom and Pop" specialty markets and stores are still holding their own.

Our First Parttime Jobs

Probably the earliest part-time job you could get as a kid growing up in Highbridge was as a newspaper delivery boy for The Bronx Home News.

I have no really clear recollection of this job, since I never did it, although many of the neighborhood kids I knew gave it a try when they were about ten or twelve years old. The Bronx Home News operated out of a storefront on 168th Street a block from my grandmother's apartment. The day's paper would be delivered there by truck from their composing and printing location and the paper boys would pick up the amount needed for their customers, stuff them in a canvas sack that could be carried over the shoulder, and walk their assigned delivery route. There were no bicycles used as there would have been out in the suburbs. No, these were walking routes and involved climbing five flights of stairs in each apartment house on your route and leaving the paper on the hallway floor in front of the apartment door of the customer.

I seem to recall this was an afternoon paper, so as soon as kids went home and dropped off their books and changed their clothes after school, they would go to the storefront to get their papers. I am a bit fuzzy about how they got paid, but I am pretty sure that it was not part of the job for them to collect from their customers by the week or month. There is one thing I do remember with certainty. Nobody ever seemed to last in the job more than a couple of weeks before they gave it up, so maybe they weren't getting paid as they were supposed to.

Once we became young teenagers, the job of choice was usually grocery delivery boy. The Empire Food Store employed delivery boys, provided them with pushcarts or bikes with big boxes on them, and sent them out to make grocery deliveries to houses as much as six or eight blocks away. As time went by, you would become very familiar with regular customers and where they lived. A customer might have half a dozen grocery bags in her order and live on the top floor of her apartment house.

We would go into the basement of the customer's building and locate which dumbwaiter shaft serviced which apartments. Let's say the manager wrote Apartment 5-C on all of her grocery bags. You would walk around that basement until you found the right dumbwaiter shaft, in this case probably C-D meaning it serviced the C and D apartments on each floor of the building. You pushed the buzzer for 5-C (just like the super did when he was collecting garbage) and when a dumbwaiter door opened up above and someone yelled "Yes?" you would announce yourself with "Grocery delivery… Empire Market" and she would tell you to send it up. Loading all her bags on the two levels of the dumbwaiter, it was time to pull the rope hand over hand and watch her order disappear up the shaft.

When the customer yelled "O.K.", you waited while the order was taken off and probably placed on the kitchen table. If an order required both levels of the dumbwaiter, you would hear something like, "Bring it up a little" and, finally, "O.K., we're done. I put a little something on there for you. Thanks for getting it here so quickly." Bringing the dumbwaiter back down, there would be a couple of coins wrapped in a piece of tissue or toilet paper. (The world had not gone crazy with paper towels yet.) The tip sent down could be anything from a quarter to a half dollar, and sometimes you got stiffed with a cookie or two. No quick delivery for her next time. In between the deliveries, you would sweep floors, clean the front door glass and the front windows, stock shelves, and straighten up the stock room. If you showed promise, the owner might even let you start to build the canned goods displays in the front windows of the store.

Our work options improved a great deal when we turned fourteen (?) and could get our Working Papers from the City or New York State. I forget who was the issuing body for working papers, perhaps the Health Department. Now, you could get a better paying job stocking shelves at the local Safeway, Grand Union, or A&P doing all the things you learned at the Empire, without home deliveries, and learning some additional things like grinding coffee, cutting, wrapping, and weighing cheese, trimming vegetables, etc. depending on which department the store manager assigned you. At this point, you could also be made a cashier and be responsible to have a balanced register tray at the end of the workday. The big chain grocery stores had register tapes, so no quick addition and grease pencil had to be involved.

63

Working papers were needed to be hired by almost anybody until you reached the age of eighteen. To get your papers, you had to go to the Bronx County Courthouse with proof of age (birth certificate or original Baptism Certificate), a letter from your school principal or a G.O. card or recent report card to prove school attendance and necessary information on who was going to hire you. Since the papers wound up going to your employer, you had to go through this process all over again every time you decided to change jobs.

With each additional year and growth in size and strength, additional jobs opened up to city youngsters. We could sell peanuts, popcorn, and hot dogs at Yankee Stadium or the Polo Grounds, both of which were an easy walk from any part of our neighborhood. Couldn't be the beer man yet… until you turned eighteen, the legal age in New York to buy beer and alcohol and work in a bar or liquor store. Becoming an usher at one of the local movie houses meant you had to look big enough and act tough enough to tell people to get their feet down off the seatback in front of them or to stop throwing rolled up candy wrappers or eject someone from the theater for sneaking in an exit door or for continuing to behave badly after being put on notice.

Since it became necessary to commute by bus or subway to most of the high schools we attended, we started taking after-school and weekend jobs out of the immediate neighborhood as we progressed through school. There were any number of varieties of part-time jobs available in downtown New York from big companies and office buildings to any of the large and famous retailers, theaters, hotels, and newspapers.

One of the really good jobs I had was as a messenger for Red Arrow Bonded Messenger Service. The garage and office were on 57th Street just off Broadway right next to Carnegie Hall. As a "newbie", I special delivered packages, envelopes, and such by train, bus, and taxi all over the city and far out into the suburbs. When I became more senior, I pedaled a bike with a stainless steel lockbox on the front of it, delivering any number of really valuable items to the rich and famous in their hotels, theaters and high rent apartments and private homes in some of the very best neighborhoods of the city.

One winter, as the business day was coming to a close and late afternoon darkness was coming on, I was pedaling my box bike up Broadway less than a block below Times Square when I was hit from behind and flipped over a car parked at the curb. Some good Samaritans helped get me into a car with my head covered with blood, despite my protest that I had valuables in the lockbox (fur coats destined for Bergdorf Goodman) and couldn't leave it. They took me off to New York Polyclinic Hospital, where I got sewed up by the best ER guys in the city. Polyclinic was right across the street from the old Madison Square Garden and they got all the hockey players, boxers, basketball players, and rodeo cowboys to practice their suturing on.

As it turned out, the rodeo was in town that week and while they worked on my lacerations, we listened to Gene Autry singing on the loudspeakers across the street. My boss showed up (another messenger came across my battered bike and recognized my gloves in the box) and took me home to the Bronx by taxi. Turned out that in my stressed-out state, the box was not locked and there was nothing in it other than my gloves. In my confusion and trauma, I didn't remember that my cargo, the expensive fur coats, had already been delivered to Bergdorf-Goodman, one of the most exclusive retailers in Manhattan, just a short time before my accident.

So, these were the kinds of run-of-the-mill, ordinary jobs a kid could work at after school and on Saturdays growing up in the city. As we grew older, stronger, and smarter, the job opportunities got even better. I'll leave it there for now, but in a later chapter, I'll describe the very best jobs a guy could have in New York City in the late 1940s and through the 1950s.

People Who Came to Our House

The Great Depression started with Black Friday in November of 1929. That was seven years before I was born, but the effect on our nation's economy would still be felt at the end of World War II when I was ten years old. It was a depression of epic proportions. It became so much a part of the fabric of the lives of the average American during the entire decade of the 1930s that it took the entire length of a four-year-long world war to finally lose its grip on our economy and allow a recovery. As millions of servicemen began returning from the European and Pacific theaters, their needs for homes and appliances and clothing led the recovery more than all the industry that had come into being to build tanks, guns, planes, and ships.

During these tough years, vagrants would knock on apartment house doors and ask if you could spare something to eat. I haven't the slightest idea how often these people met with rejection, but if my mom was in the midst of preparing supper for the family, she would be more than happy to prepare a bowl of soup or stew and some bread or a roll and serve it to him while he sat on the stairs in the hallway. Many of my friends had parents who were easy touches, as well, and it was by no means an uncommon occurrence even as late as the end of the second world war.

Another frequent neighborhood visitor who sometimes came by was the courtyard singer or musician. These fellows would suddenly start singing a cappella in the rear courtyard between two apartment houses. Sometimes he was not a singer but would play several musical selections on a violin, fiddle, saxophone, or accordion. After several selections, apartment dwellers would reward his efforts to provide us some entertainment by throwing some coins wrapped in tissue or toilet paper into the courtyard or air shaft. He would shout out a "Thank You", pick up his money and move on to the next courtyard.

During these years, it was not uncommon to see horse-drawn wagons still coming up the avenue, with various services being offered by tradesmen. The most common of these were fruit and vegetable peddlers, junk men collecting anything you might want to get rid of, and tool and knife sharpeners. The latter tradesman had a grinding wheel in his wagon to put a sharpened edge on anything that needed it. All of these guys had a variety of bells on their carts to announce their approach and all of them yelled out, "Pots and pans" or "Knives sharpened" or whatever other services they were offering in a loud singsong voice. In the later years of my growing up in the Bronx, there would be ice cream vendors like Good Humor or Bungalow Bar, or Mr. Softee. Sometimes even a truck with a cage on the back that contained some kind of miniature carnival ride. Their attention-getting shouts or singing can still be heard in my head today as I write these memories.

Insurance men from various, well-known insurance companies were very common in the neighborhood. They wore suits and ties and walked the streets collecting premiums from their customers. To this day, I cannot understand how they survived or managed to stay so professional looking. Their territory was called a "debit" and they called on many of the clients who made up their debit as frequently as once a week collecting premiums that amounted to a few coins to pay for policies that might typically be for $500 or $1,000.

Other visitors to the neighborhood were the door to door salesmen. The suburbs probably had their share of these, but the city, with its density of population, was a treasure trove of sales opportunities for them. Magazine subscription sales were close to the forefront of this activity, but just about any kind of household product might be in his sample bag. Of course, the best known of the door to door salesmen was the Fuller Brush man. The sample bag they hauled around contained any kind of brush you could think of from hairbrushes to scrub brushes to vegetable brushes to toothbrushes.

The photo on the previous page depicts "Funny man Red Skelton" in a Hollywood movie comedy titled "The Fuller Brush Man." After filling out your order form, they usually got
upfront paid upfront and would deliver all the brushes you ordered the following week. Some of these door-to-door salespeople must have done pretty well as many of them remained on their route for years and were known by name.

The Housing Authority in New York City controlled and looked out for tenants' rights and legislated the standards of how landlords had to maintain their apartment houses. One of the rights in every tenant's lease was to have his apartment painted every four years. A notice would be put up near the mailboxes under the stairs announcing the coming appearance of "the painters" during such and such days or weeks. Soon afterward, a crew chief would come by to meet with each housewife to see which color they wanted for each room. Your choice of colors was limited to about eight or ten basic colors. Yellow, blue, green, white, pink.... whatever you chose, it came straight out of the can, the exact same shade of yellow, blue, green that any of your neighbors might choose for their room colors. Think Crayola crayons basic box of eight primary colors.

A painting crew of two or three would knock out an apartment in a day and a half or two days. They moved and covered your furniture in the middle of each room and did ceilings, walls, doors, window frames, and baseboards and were on their way and would return again in four years. You could smell fresh paint drying throughout the building. When that smell was gone, you knew the painters had finished their last apartment and moved along to the next address on their list.

Coal deliveries were a common event in the neighborhood. The truck would back up partially onto the sidewalk and extend a coal chute into a covered hatch in the front of the building. The hatch led to the coal bunker in the basement and when the back of the truck was raised the coal would rush down the chute and disappear into the front of the apartment house. A helper in the truck finished off at the end by climbing around the slanted back of the truck, cleaning out the corners… first with a coal shovel and then with a broom. Occasionally some pieces of coal had to be picked up off the sidewalk when they were finished, but for the most part, these drivers were artists, raising the backs of their trucks just fast enough to facilitate the coal going down the chute at the perfect speed and volume. While buildings were receiving their coal delivery, pedestrian traffic was disrupted on the sidewalk and people had to walk around the front of the truck in the street, where vehicular traffic was also affected by the nose of the truck extending into the traffic lane. Of course, the day would come when oil delivery trucks would replace the coal trucks. They were nowhere near as interesting and fun to watch.

I mentioned earlier about the garbage and cinder pick-ups by the sanitation trucks. These same trucks did snow removal when it became necessary, but another interesting aspect of neighborhood life was the street cleaner. Most of the time he worked entirely alone and was probably a holdover from the horse and wagon era when their offered services were even more necessary. These guys sort of disappeared in the early 40's when just about everything in the city became mechanized and manure was no longer the pedestrian's nightmare.

It's hard to believe, but there was a time when you waited with your name on a list until the Bell Telephone Company sent an installer to your apartment to finally connect you to modern communications with your friends and loved ones. And, if you were a typical family, you probably went through the whole installation process just a few years later when your folks finally bought that Philco, Admiral, or Motorola television console. It was an event to watch the phone man wiring up that rotary dial black phone. When the TV went in, it might have been a one-man operation or he might have had a helper, as you now had to find a suitable spot up on the roof of the apartment house for your antenna and have a coaxial cable run down the side of your building and across one of your window sills.

I'm sure many others came to our house (or neighborhood) but this group of people are the ones I remember most vividly, including that when the TV installer was finally gone, if you were one of the earliest families to have one, you would probably see a lot of visitors coming to your apartment for a while to watch a show or just ooh and ahh at the wonder of it all.

The Candy Store & the Neighborhood Bar

In my freshman year at Iona College, I had an economics professor who came from some European country complete with a thick accent. He was full of his so very pithy comments concerning economics in America and New York City in particular. One of the first of these pronouncements he dropped on us was: "The primary economy of the Bronx is a candy store on every corner and a bar in the middle of the block." As a lifelong resident of the Bronx, I found his attempt at humor at our expense a little off-putting.... but it got me thinking and I found I couldn't completely disagree with his proclamation. No matter what mix of stores and businesses existed where you lived, the heart of the neighborhood and the social gathering places were the candy stores and the bars.

On the block where I grew up, Duskin's candy store was just five or six stores up the street from our apartment house. I don't think we ever knew the first names of this elderly Jewish couple; they were always Mr. Duskin and Mrs. Duskin. What made Duskin's noteworthy was that it was located on our side of the street at a time when we were forbidden to cross the street without one of our parents. So during our earliest years, Duskin's became our candy store of choice. Right across Ogden Avenue from Duskin's was Charlie's, which would eventually become Lester's, Harry's, and then Tootsie's or Clark's. Eventually, we reached an age where we were allowed to cross the street with any grown-up: "Lady, can you cross me?" Now we had Charlie's, Lester's, and Tootsie's as an alternative to Duskins. Most pedestrians were kind enough to interrupt their travels, take you by the hand, and lead you to the other side. Of course, you knew a lot of the regular residents in your area, too, and that always helped in finding a "crosser". While I'm on the subject of crossing the street, there was sometimes one more level to go through. If your apartment was in the front of the building with windows facing the street, there came a time when you could stand on the sidewalk in front of the house and yell, "Ma, can you cross me?" and she would watch up and down the street and, while you had your head on a swivel checking her timing and yours, she would say go and you'd make it across without a hand holder.

Most candy stores had the same basic attractions; Penny-candy, gum, and well-known candy bars (usually in glass display cases). Plus they had a soda fountain and ice cream selections for anything from penny Vichy (seltzer water) to ice cream sodas, "black and whites" and Egg Creams (a New York favorite).

In my neighborhood, another favorite was lemon and lime with water. That meant you didn't want it with seltzer. Other "must-haves" for any good candy store were a well-stocked magazine section with all the latest comic books and magazines like Life, Look, People, Esquire, and The Saturday Evening Post. Esquire was the Playboy of those years, complete with a scantily clad model in the centerfold long before Playboy came along with full nudity in the centerfold. God forbid your mother should find a couple of editions of Esquire under your bed.

Cigarettes, cigars, pipe tobacco, photo film, and flashbulbs were also available as were cheap toy items such as kites (fly 'em in the lot or park or from your apartment house roof), yo-yo's (use them anywhere), and the one mentioned in an earlier chapter, the pink, high-bounce Spauldeen. Rounding out the list of things that made for a good candy store was a payphone in a booth with a folding door for privacy. What a concept, actually wanting privacy for a phone call instead of having twenty people listening in to your cell phone conversation. Finally, a booth or two for eating your dish of ice cream, Sundae, or banana split with your friends was another plus, if space allowed.

Another thing that made the candy store the social gathering spot of the neighborhood was a well-stocked comic book rack that attracted the kids. As one of those kids, I remember Lester or Duskin shouting, "Are you kids going to buy one of those comics or just keep looking until the ink wears off the pages?"

And, every candy store had a newspaper stand out front on the sidewalk. This was where the adults (usually men) gathered to await the latest edition of their favorite newspaper. The stand was just a roll-around box counter, large enough on top to display six stacks of papers, usually the Daily News, the Mirror, Journal-American, Wall Street Journal, and whatever other newspaper was in vogue at the time. Some of these papers had three or four editions a day. There might be a morning edition, afternoon edition, and the Five Star Final in the early evening. A small knot of neighborhood "news junkies" would stand around waiting for their favorite paper truck to come up the street, stop briefly and drop a stack of newspapers on the curb. Sometimes the candy store owner couldn't even get outside fast enough to pick up the delivered stack. One of the men waiting might lift the stack up on the newspaper stand, cut the string tying up the bundle, drop his nickel or dime on the stand and head off with his paper, the other news junkies quickly following his lead. All Mr. Duskin or Lester had to do was go outside periodically to collect the money their newspaper customers left on the stand. Until television came of age, these newspapers were the primary disseminators of the latest news. Radio broadcast news couldn't hold a visual candle to today's television news programs, but if you wanted to view your news stories on "The Big Screen," you could go to the local movie theater once or twice a week to see ten or twelve minutes of recent news stories in film format between the two featured movies and a cartoon or two.

Everyone had their own favorite neighborhood bar. Almost every one of them had a touch of the "Cheers" camaraderie for the particular group that found it to their liking. Some felt comfortable in all of them. The most popular watering hole on our block for my father and his cronies was really not a bar at all. It was a Jewish Delicatessen right next door to Duskins candy store and it didn't look anything like the "Cheers" we watched on TV for years. With a marble tile floor, plain tables along the length of one wall, and bentwood chairs at those tables, they served up the most delicious pastrami and corned beef sandwiches, kosher hot dogs and potato salad, coleslaw, and sour pickles. The other wall had a bar in the front half and the food preparation area towards the rear. Beer on tap and basic whiskey for "shots" were the hallmark of the "deli", which in my younger years was known as Diamonds and later became Julie's. My father and his pals, a couple of cops, a fireman, a construction worker, and a construction crane operator, would stop in "for a few" most days on their way home from work. An eclectic group to be sure, they followed this ritual for many years.

In the days before we had our own phone, we used to give out the Deli's public phone number as our own. Max Diamond would walk about a hundred feet down the street and call up to our front window on the second floor: "Lester, there's a call for you in the store."

We would yell back, "OK, tell them we'll be right there."

Up the street from Diamond's (later Julie's), was the Harp and Eagle, a quiet, cool, dark bar frequented by elderly gentlemen and neighborhood mothers taking a break from pushing their baby carriages in mid-afternoon to relax together in a booth and have a cold beer on tap or a soda. Rounding out the bars on our block was the Blarney Stone, a little 'grittier' than the others already mentioned and a favored hang-out of the younger, wilder members of our neighborhood. It wasn't exactly "a bucket of blood", but if a fight were going to break out in one of the bars on our street, chances are it would be the Blarney Stone.

There was one more local watering hole just around the corner from our block. It was the Edward L. Grant Post of the American Legion (Post #1225) and deserves a chapter all its own a little later on in this narrative.

I guess you can see for yourself that Dr. Chudoba wasn't as wrong as I initially thought when he described his vision of the economy of the Bronx.

Up on the Rooftop

When you wanted to get away from the hustle and
bustle on the sidewalk, you could always find some peace
and quiet up on the roof, five floors above the noise of the
street down below. The apartment house roof served a
wide variety of uses depending on who you were.
Probably the most important use for the younger
occupants of the building came during the summer
months when the roof became known as "Tar Beach".

Just put on a bathing suit, apply some suntan oil
(nobody had ever heard of sunscreen), grab a blanket or
bath towel to spread on the tarred surface of the roof and
you were ready to work on your tan. It was a reasonable
substitute for taking a bus or subway to a beach that might
be an hour or more away. Add some snacks, sunglasses,

portable radio, plus a folding canvas chair and you had it all.

I must confess I was not a tar beach guy. I was fortunate enough to have parents who had a vacation bungalow away from the blistering heat of the city in the summer months, I did not learn what tar beach was until the summer of '52 when I turned 16 and stayed in the city to work as an NYC Parks Department lifeguard. Until that very enlightening summer, I never realized how hot and oppressive the city could get. My mom usually pulled us out of school about the second week of June when exams were finished and the nuns, brothers and lay teachers were just babysitting their classes to get the full school year in. We never once returned to the Bronx until the day after Labor Day and I spent my days playing baseball, swimming, fishing, boating, picking blackberries, and catching turtles for an idyllic twelve weeks or so. As much as I thought I fully appreciated how great those summers were, it wasn't until the summer of 1952 that I understood how lucky I'd been to have such beautiful fun-filled summers away from the blistering heat of summertime in the city.

In a departure from the timetable I outlined above, my mother did return to the city early that year to give birth to my brother, Russell, on August 1st., but I'm almost sure she got back to the bungalow for a little more time with her newborn before the Labor Day weekend brought us back to Highbridge.

In any season of the year, the buildings' roofs lent themselves to games such as hide and seek, ring-o-levio, war games, and such, where you could run from one apartment house roof to another, gain entry to the stairs and hallway of another house and expand a "playing field" boundaries to a whole block and five or six connected apartment houses. And when the winter snows started falling, there was no better place to launch a snowball attack than five stories above the sidewalks. Got someone you needed to get even with for some reason? Get two or three buddies with three or four snowballs each, wait for your target, and launch. Working quickly and with a little luck, you could have eight to twelve snowballs on their way to target before the first one even hit. Good stuff!!

A few other uses for the roof-tops would begin first with clotheslines for drying your wash. If your apartment had a window on the courtyard between buildings, you would install a clothesline on two pulleys across to a window in the next building and you could put items on the line to dry right from your own apartment. However, if you had only windows with nothing across from them to attach a drying line to, you were welcome to take your laundry up to the roof and use the clotheslines there. Sometimes, you could find a roof-top vegetable garden consisting of large pots of soil with tomatoes and other veggies growing in them. To the best of my knowledge, these bucolic efforts at city farming were, for the most part, universally respected by all and the apartment dwelling farmers usually got to eat the fruits of their labors.

The final metamorphosis of the city roof-top began around 1950 with the advent of affordable, if small, black and white television sets. As one after another apartment dweller finally satisfied their dream to have their own set, another wire ran up the side of the building to a roof-top TV antenna.

The cable that connected the television set in your apartment to the antenna up on the roof was a flat, thin sort of thing like a ribbon rather than the round cables so prevalent for today's electronics. This made it very simple to tack it across your window sill and still be able to close and lock the window.

The Apartment-House Basement

In an earlier segment, I reminisced about the apartment house roof, aka Tar Beach. Now, allow me to introduce you to the apartment house basement. The cellar, as we called it, in many ways was just like the basement in your private dwelling today. You have somewhere in your basement, a heating unit of some kind and probably one or more air conditioning units, which would not have been in a New York apartment building in the middle of the last century. When I was growing up, and before my teenage years, our apartment house basement held a large coal-burning furnace and elsewhere a supply of coal in a bunker accessible to the sidewalk in the front of the building so that the coal trucks could make their deliveries down a chute and into the bunker. It was the responsibility of the superintendent or his family to keep the furnace stoked with coal during cold months and to remove the burnt cinders after they cooled. But of equal importance, water levels had to be maintained, both for hot water supply to the families in the house and for the steam that traveled through pipes and radiators to keep the tenants warm in their apartments. As I grew through my early teens, oil and oil delivery trucks started to replace coal as the fuel source of choice, but almost all other chores of the "super" remained pretty much the same. One big change that probably made every apartment house superintendent ecstatic was the elimination of the need to carry all those barrels of cinders up out of the basement for curbside pick-up.

Most Bronx apartments were very tight on living space and closets were not spacious or plentiful. Apartment dwellers were very adept at storing things under every bed in the house, behind larger pieces of furniture, and in every nook and cranny of closets where clothes were not hanging and in every corner of kitchen cabinets that didn't have dishes, glassware, and food items in them. There was a box with a door in it about a cubic foot in size under the window in the kitchen. These had been included in the original designs of apartment houses as a place to keep an extra block of ice for the iceboxes that were the only means of cooling and refrigeration when these buildings were built. By the time I reached school age, less and less people were still using ice and the Frigidaire came into its own. That little box under the kitchen window became the primary storage area for household cleaners, shoe polish, rags, and any non-food item that would fit in it. It was also the preferred entry point for roaches so it was the first place to get a big spray of bug juice when you had finally "had it" and decided to "go to the mattresses" with the little devils.

If you simply had to have more closet space for coats, dresses, and suits, you could buy a piece of furniture called a chifferobe, which was nothing more than another closet in a cabinet similar to today's armoire. One more thing before we get back to the cellar of the building. My dad and my uncle built faux fireplaces to stand in the living room with electric logs and andirons to make the appearance of living in a single-family home in the suburbs. They had nice molding and fake bricks and the six square feet or so of space they took was not a total loss. Inside, or behind, each make-believe fireplace was just enough room to store all the Christmas tree ornaments, lights, etc. from one winter to the next.

But getting back to the basement... there was a labyrinth of concrete passages and rooms down there. Not cinder block, which hadn't been developed yet, but poured concrete usually kept whitewashed by the super. In one or more of these concrete rooms, the families of the house would store the larger things that couldn't fit upstairs in the apartments or were too ungainly to get up the hallway stairs. Baby carriages, strollers, and coaches were the main storage items, but bikes and tricycles were right up there also. These cave-like storage rooms were sometimes packed wall to wall and a lot of jockeying was usually necessary to get your carriage into the passageway and out into the courtyard to pull it up ten or twelve steps to the sidewalk level.

There were seldom any doors let alone locks on the apartment house basement storage rooms, but very few incidences were ever heard about things being stolen out of these communal storerooms. Although space was usually at a premium in the cellar, sometimes there was some to spare. A friend of mine was a highly skilled cabinet and furniture maker and he got his building superintendent to rent him space for a woodworking shop in an unused area which he closed off to all the other tenants with a locked door (which he built) to protect his tools and his projects. It was a terrific second income to him during his early married years.

With the advent of automatic washing machines, coin laundromats began opening for business in many neighborhoods and once it became obvious that this new modern convenience was here to stay, landlords began having their superintendents install one or two of them in apartment house cellars. Since the development of the accompanying dryers was still to come, there came a period when the family's clothes were washed in the basement and carried up to your apartment to be hung out on a clothesline from your kitchen window to a neighbor's across the courtyard. If it was too big a wash for your clothesline you could always carry it in a wicker basket up five or six flights of stairs to the roof to be hung out to dry up there. If another family's clothes were still on the lines, but already dry, your mom would be upset that somebody was hogging the drying time (sunny, daylight hours) and not checking their wash in a timely fashion.

The baby carriages that were stored in the basements of your neighborhood were typically large, ornate, and expensive. Sure, you could still see canvas or cloth folding strollers for summer use for older babies, but nothing as small and portable as some of the models you see today that look like two umbrellas when they're folded up. The bigger carriages I'm referring to were sometimes called coaches... and like Cinderella's ride to the ball, they were all of that. Of course, they were heavy, so the mom's had a real job jockeying everyone else's coach around to get theirs out and then pulling it up ten or twelve steps (with the baby in it) to street level.

The picture here shows our daughter, Leslie, in a carriage we called "the Pope-mobile" years before the pontiff rode around in a vehicle that the Italian paparazzi had christened with the same name. Note the painted and lacquered sides and the fine "Corinthian leather", the heavy-duty springs, undercarriage, and parking brake. The frosting on the cake was that we lived in those apartment houses across the street in this picture and they had street level, walk-out storage, and basements.

I realize I got a little far afield from the apartment house basement in this installment, but the storage and closet space in a typical apartment had to be an integral part of telling the story of basement storage rooms and the big baby coaches that were in vogue had to be brought to the readers' attention to underline the challenges that faced young mothers of the day and the trust in the basic honesty of others to put expensive pieces of equipment in a common storage room with no locks. Was this the kind of place you would feel safe to live and grow up in…. you bet it was. And that even included the dark, mysterious cellar of that big apartment house you called home.

The Matron

When we speak of someone being a matron in the present-day concept, we would normally have a consensus from any mixed group of people that a matron is an older woman, possibly one who is well-off financially, sophisticated, and, possibly a little imperious and dominant.

The matron of the 1940s and 1950s was a job title and carried with it a good deal of authority and power, especially over kids up through "middle school" age. She would have been thought of as "The Matron" in a similar way to how kids would refer to The Super or The Cops.

Kids growing up in the city spent a lot of time at the neighborhood movie house. All the way through the 1940s, there was still no television to amuse them and all the electronic games, i-pads and phones that they can't live without today would have been fantasies if we could have even conceived of them. Serials on the radio (The Lone Ranger, Captain Sky King, The Shadow, etc.) were OK, as were the ever-present comic books, but the "real" entertainment action took place in your local movie house. The most visible manifestation of the "matron" was here, in movie houses that were sometimes independents, but most frequently chains owned by Loews or RKO theaters. And there were no Cineplexes... there was one double feature playing for three or four days and then the offering would change for the balance of the week.

The Matron was the "mall security cop" of the mid-century. She may have had a couple of high school-age ushers to assist her (the bigger the better) but make no mistake about it... the Matron was in charge. She and the other ushers swept up and down the aisles regularly and made sure you didn't have your feet up on the seatback of the row in front of you. They also made sure the boys weren't bothering the girls. Plus, they checked to see that nobody underage was smoking in the restrooms. The Matron wore a white uniform like the nurses of the era and she struck terror into the hearts of anyone considering getting out of order. If you threw balled up candy wrappers at kids in the rows ahead of you, she would catch you eventually and you would be unceremoniously removed from the theater. The same result would come from flicking the silver foil inner wraps from chewing gum packages up through the path of the projected image. This would result in something that looked like a shooting star and could lead to other gum chewers joining in if she didn't track the offender quickly enough to avoid a miniature meteor shower.

Some kids would pool their money and send in one of them with a paid admission ticket, then as soon as conditions looked favorable, he would open one of the exit doors and the others would rush into the movie house and scatter staying low and moving quickly. The object was to crawl into a seat and look like you had been there since the picture started. In this instance, the younger ushers who were faster than her would usually be the ones to try to track down the gate-crashers. Such was the job of the Matron and her staff of ushers. Pictured here is my neighborhood movie house, the Ogden, where I spent many Saturdays enjoying a double feature and 10 or more cartoons under the watchful eye of the Matron and her staff.

Another kind of matron worked in the "comfort station" just up the street from the Ogden movie house. The Comfort Station was a public restroom and waiting room on the Bronx end of the old Washington Bridge. The building was marble and granite like the bridge itself and was kept immaculately clean by the matron in attendance. It served as a waiting room for the trolleys, later buses, that came across the bridge from Manhattan, but anyone was welcome to come in and sit down and rest awhile on the oak benches to get in out of the heat of summer or the chill of winter. To say that the comfort station was clean would be a gross understatement. There was never a time that the comfort station was not only immaculately kept but also smelled as if the marble and granite floors had just dried after a cleaning. The worst it would ever look would be if people tracked snow and ice in on their galoshes (rubber boots) during a winter snowfall. This matron, an employee of the city or the transit company (I'm not sure which) was totally in charge of this facility and was assisted by a janitor, who spent hours mopping and cleaning a building that was probably no bigger than 1200 square feet counting the waiting room and the men's and women's toilets. All in all, picture a very miniature Grand Central Station without the ticket windows and the information kiosk.

There was a time in our family that my grandmother worked as a matron in a New York City firehouse. She cleaned up and made beds for the on-duty firemen and wore that same white uniform that the movie house matron and the comfort station matron wore. There were a couple of times that I went with her to that firehouse in the south Bronx if she was watching me for some reason for my folks, but I was too young to even think of asking if she worked for the city, the Fire Department or the firemen of that particular firehouse. My grandfather, her husband, had been a New York City fireman before he died and left a sizeable family of seven. In retrospect, I've wondered if this job was the FDNY's way of taking care of its own. I have no memory of whether that job included cooking for the guys in that station or if she even worked a full day. And that was the matrons of my youth as I remember them. As you can see from these descriptions, the term "matron" had a completely different connotation in my day. They were blue-collar workers, Not Park Avenue dowagers.

The Very Best Teenage Jobs in the City

At the closing of Chapter 6, where I reminisced about our first jobs while growing up in the Bronx, I mentioned that in a later chapter I would tell of the absolute very best jobs a young guy could have in the city.

While it was great to finally be old enough to work and earn some money for our- selves, the jobs that commonly

NEW YORK GIANTS - NATIONAL LEAGUE CHAMPIONS - MIRACLE TEAM 1951

existed were things like newspaper delivery boy, grocery store stock clerk and grocery delivery boys and things of that nature, which were all covered pretty extensively in that chapter.

But there did exist a handful of jobs that were the Holy Grail of jobs for coming of age teenagers. There was one which was well beyond the pale of the average day-dreaming city kid… about as likely to happen as having a

95

date with a movie starlet. This one was such a reach and had so few openings, I would not under ordinary circumstances, think to even mention it, but a cousin of mine had that job… batboy for the New York Giants. Between the Giants and the Yankees, only a couple of kids held those jobs. My cousin, once removed, Billy Leonard, was the visiting team batboy with the Giants from about age 13 to age 16. He got to shag fly balls with the team in pre-game batting practice, had a complete set of uniforms for every national league team, and got to share a dug-out with all the league's baseball greats during those years. But the real topper was getting to be in the National League Championship team picture with the 1951 Giants. That's Bill in the very front of the picture with manager Leo Durocher right behind him. Unfortunately, there was a height limit for their batboys, so Bill was done in by Wonder Bread, which "built strong bodies 8 ways" before he even got through high school.

I did get to be what most Bronx kids would have considered "the best job in the city" since being a Yankee or Giants batboy was just beyond any normal guy's ability to even have in the mix. I became an NYC Department of Parks lifeguard and was assigned to Orchard Beach in Pelham Bay Park on Long Island Sound.

Fifty-one lifeguards manned towers (or lifeguard chairs) on 17 sections covering a mile and a tenth along the tranquil waters of the sound. In the midst of a really bad summer heatwave or on a July Fourth or Labor Day weekend, it was not unusual to have 100,000 to 200,000 people on that one mile. We would sometimes be the big story of the day with a full-page aerial photo on the front of the Daily News or the Mirror. If low tide fell at a particularly bad time of day on such a weekend, it was not unusual for guards on the busiest sections to run up totals of 25, 35, or even more rescues by the time we went off duty in the late afternoon or evening.

The City of New York gave us one day a week off and it had to be a weekday, so we worked 6 eight-hour days for the princely sum of $72.00 per week. Although that might seem like a ridiculous amount of money, remember this was the 1950's and, if we did some smart money management, we would have a pretty good bank role towards our Fall semester tuition and book bills, which were also ridiculously low when viewed against today's college costs.

Les, Mickey, Tony, and Phil are pictured enjoying some quiet time before the tide went out and things started to get busy. Then the word would be passed down the beach, "Everybody up. All breaks are canceled" and we would start earning that $72.00 a week. As the tide receded it reached a line where there was a ledge or drop- off under the water about six to ten feet out from the water's edge. There were also some underwater holes that swimmers could step into that could change location from week to week due to the action of the tides. Notice in the photo above that three of the four guards pictured are wearing miraculous medals or Saint Christopher medals, not something you often see today.

Just about any guy in New York would have loved to have this ideal summer job if only he could pass the Department of Parks training program held every winter in their 54th Street pool off Second Avenue in Manhattan. Those who were able to pass the course found themselves in a job where they could luxuriate all day in the sun, meet all the girls they could ever dream of, and have them bringing them great lunches regularly. At any bus stop along Fordham Road or Moshulu Parkway, we went straight to the front of the long lines of beach-goers waiting for the bus to the beach and boarded first by just waving our lifeguard whistles and locker keys to the driver or the starter (who was there to keep order in the line)

I worked with one lifeguard partner for a short time one summer, who had two of the city's best jobs for a guy growing up in New York.

During the summer he was a lifeguard and in the winter he was an ice-rink attendant at the Wohlman Memorial Ice Skating Rink in Central Park. That was the rink that became a New York City boondoggle when the city couldn't seem to get it repaired and back in use and had to close it for six years. It was supposed to be a 2-year project and cost 9.5 million dollars, but after six years of no progress, Donald Trump told the mayor that he could fix the problems in three months for three million dollars. It was ready for use that winter and came in 25% under budget.

In addition to the Central Park rink, the city also had ice skating rinks and some lakes available in the outlying boroughs, where a guy could get that job, but overall, there were nowhere near the opportunities that summer lifeguarding could provide. Of course, if a skater couldn't get one of those prime ice skating jobs, there was always the chance for a roller skating rink job. There were a goodly number of those available in every one of the five boroughs, as it was a very popular activity for kids who grew up with steel sidewalk skates and were anxious to see how good they were with "shoe" skates and roller bearing wheels.

Above, Rocky and Adrian skate in an ice skating rink in a scene from "Rocky." Well, she's skating, he's sliding. Both roller and skating rinks were very popular in the city at the time I was growing up.

Neighborhood & First Run Movie Theaters

When Hollywood releases a new film today, it opens in theaters all over the country at the same time and is always billed as a spectacular or blockbuster or Academy Award nominee. Given enough ballyhoo to bring out the masses on the opening weekend, there's a good chance the movie makers will know if it's a financial success or a dud after that first opening weekend.

When I was growing up in the Bronx, every major motion picture had its opening in the downtown area of the city in one of the major theaters of the Times Square, Broadway, or 42nd Street area. That picture would continue to play in only that one showcase theater for several weeks before moving out to the neighborhood movie houses of Brooklyn, Queens and the Bronx, and the rest of the country. While they were in the downtown "first-run" theaters such as the Paramount, Radio City Music Hall, or the Roxy, they didn't have a second movie with them but would have stage shows as part of each showing.

The Roxy was the original home of the famous dance troupe, the Rockettes and the big attraction at Radio City Music Hall was the world-famous "Mighty Wurlitzer" organ. Naturally, an organ recital would take center stage in between showings of the new movie at Radio City. The movies shown at the Paramount Theater were the new releases of Paramount Studios and were frequently accompanied by live stage shows featuring the stars of the current film. You might be treated to a little stand-up comedy by Bob Hope, Bing Crosby, and Dorothy Lamour if the latest offering was a "Road" picture.

101

Those three performers starred in close to a dozen "Road" movies. Road to Utopia, Road to Morocco, Road to Bali, and Road to Zanzibar to name a few.

Dean Martin and Jerry Lewis, at the height of their popularity, would make it necessary for the NYPD to put a lot of extra cops in Times Square to control the crowds of young admirers, many "playing hooky", that would swarm the area and, of course, the same would be true if a Frank Sinatra musical was accompanied by a few songs on stage by Frank, himself. The first "swoon" at a Sinatra appearance took place in the aisle of the Paramount Theater. The Paramount boasted over 3,600 seats and during the 40's it helped energize the "swing era" showcasing all the famous bands and musicians of the day along with its first run feature presentation. The Beatles ended their first USA tour at the Paramount with a massive turnout of their fans filling the streets enough to impede traffic through Times Square.

The Rockettes, whom I mentioned previously, had started their New York City identity as the "Roxyettes" but eventually moved to the Music Hall as the Radio City Rockettes. They can still be seen today for free as part of the Macy's Thanksgiving Day Parade, but if you want to see their famous kick line on stage at Radio City, be prepared to shell out over $100 a ticket.

I mentioned that the Paramount had 3,600 seats. The Roxy and Radio City had over 5,900 seats each. An eighth-grader or freshman in high school would usually have earned the approval of his or her parents by that age to ride the subway to Times Square to see first-run movies at only slightly more money per ticket than they would pay several weeks later when the films came to their neighborhood movie houses. Of course, the live stage shows wouldn't come "uptown", but the featured movie would be packaged with a second film, which came to be known as a B movie, with several cartoons, a short subject or two, and a weekly edition of Movietone News. The B movie was usually a black and white film, featuring up-and-coming stars or those who were on the decline in popularity with the movie public.

As you might expect, it was not unusual to go into a local movie house at 11:00 o'clock or so on a Saturday morning and not come out until after dark and almost be late for dinner. All for 35 cents and a bit more for candy and popcorn. Just as the movie theaters had heralded the death of vaudeville, the advent of television in the early part of the 1950s was the beginning of the end for the neighborhood movie houses.

Today, we take our kids or a date to the Mega Cinamaplex, have our choice of as many as 10 or 12 features, and are back out again in two and a half hours or so. The hood of the car is still warm when we get back out to the parking lot.

When kids in Highbridge, or any other Bronx neighborhood you could name, went into the "movies" on a Saturday morning, it was the beginning of a marathon with all those features, cartoons, newsreels, coming attractions, and so forth.

There was every chance that when the feature that started it came around for the second showing, some guy would say, "Ya wanna see it again?" And, we would all say, "Yeah, might as well."

The result of spending all those many hours in the theater was somewhat akin to arriving back on earth after a long mission in outer space. Depending on the season of the year at the time, we might have the summer heat or the cold of winter smack us in the face as we emerged. If it was summer and still light out, the glare could almost make us dizzy until our pupils adjusted to the sunlight. Winters could be the worst though. It might have been a sunny, mild morning when we bought our tickets and went inside, only to exit in cold and darkness with wintry winds and a couple of inches of snow on the ground. Talk about a wake-up call.

There was one other thing about spending all that time in the movie house on a nice Saturday. If we stayed too long, there was always the possibility that your mother or older sibling would come to find you, if the family was waiting on you to arrive home to eat with the rest of the family. There was nothing more embarrassing for a guy than to have his mother in a housecoat and apron drag him up the center aisle by his ear. Especially, if he and his buddies had moved into seats around some of the neighborhood girls and were trying to impress them with some moves.

Ask any older person who grew up in the Bronx or northern Manhattan in that era, what movie houses they remember, and they will probably be able to mention a good ten or so like, The Ogden, The Crest, RKO Fordham, Loews Paradise (a national landmark today), the Coliseum, the Park Plaza, Lowes 175th Street, Lowes American, and The Lane. They were a huge part of our growing up years in the City.

The Edward L. Grant Post #1225 — American Legion

From about the time I entered Sacred Heart grammar school until I married and moved from the Highbridge neighborhood I grew up in, the "Post" was a very big part of my life. Sometimes called the Post, sometimes also referred to as "the club."

The official name was The Captain Edward L. Grant Post #1225 – American Legion and the members were proud to refer to it as "America's Baseball Post". Eddie Grant had been an infielder with the New York Giants and several other clubs for a number of seasons and he became one of the "doughboys" who went to France during World

War I. He was killed while leading his infantry company in the Meuse-Argonne forest trying to determine the location of "the Lost Battalion".

My earliest memories of the Post are of World War II, when servicemen from all branches would arrive, perhaps after a baseball or football game at Yankee Stadium or the Polo Grounds, having been told they could get a free dinner there. They had one of the smallest kitchens in the world just behind the bar and it was amazing that the two cooks could turn out the quantity of food that they did. No serviceman was ever turned away because the food ran out and the place was often full to capacity with men in the uniform of every service. I do remember that there was never a choice of menu, as the tiny kitchen was hard-pressed to turn out one meal, let alone a selection. It would usually be a full turkey dinner with all the trimmings, or ham or roast beef with all the usual vegetables you would expect. Even though food items, especially meat, were heavily rationed during the war, there never seemed to be a shortage at the Post. The G.I.'s and sailors loved the way the members welcomed them and fed them… so nobody ever questioned how or where the club got their victuals.

By the time I entered high school, I worked at the post on many weekend nights when the upstairs hall was rented out or the club was having a dance or fundraiser of its own. For a good six or seven years, I had the cloakroom concession all to myself. I worked for tips and while I did very well with outside parties and wedding receptions that booked the hall, the take on an American Legion post-dance was really terrific.

Every person in the hall knew me and wanted to help me out with tuition and textbook money. I often made more in tips for a 4 or 5-hour stint than I did in a whole week of lifeguarding in the summer. I continued in that job into my college years, becoming a waiter during the warmer months when people weren't wearing coats and hats.

Sometimes the post would play host to a Yankee or Giants affair. If a radio or field announcer or head groundskeeper or club houseman was retiring or being honored for many years of service to the Stadium or Polo Grounds, the front office would book the Eddie Grant Post for the dinner and ceremonies. I was able to meet a lot of the players, coaches, and scouts that way. Sometimes they even sent up some regular team uniforms for the waiters to wear at these team events. It was great fun for a young guy. Of course, if one of the ballplayers was being honored, that was usually held at the Concourse Plaza or one of the big downtown hotels.

When this American Legion post was chartered, it soon found it did not have enough vets to make the monthly expenses (bar, electric, maintenance, etc.) They came up with the idea of forming a Booster's Club made up of non-vets, who wanted to enjoy the benefits of a "private" type of club. My father and a number of his cronies were among the first of the "boosters" and I became one when I turned eighteen, the New York legal drinking age. Eventually, I even served a year as the president of the organization as my dad had before me. Of course, I was in college by then.

Almost from the start, the boosters outnumbered the regular veteran's group, which mostly consisted of World War I vets who were in or approaching their sixties, while the boosters were made up largely of an age group of 20 to 50-year-olds. In the earliest years of my Post memories, many of those younger boosters had jobs in the factories and shipyards that were turning out the ships and other equipment needed by those guys who flocked to the post when they could. We were the driving force behind the Post; the guys who did the money-raising to keep the club solvent. We ran a couple of dances a year, sold chances on a couple of things a year and our big event would be raffling off a new car each winter. I can remember so many chilly or snowy nights I sold chances somewhere on Fordham Road, Washington Heights, or the "Hub" all of which were major uptown shopping areas. The car would be parked up on the curb to slow down the Christmas shoppers walking by. We had a good number of the NYPD in our membership and usually could get the cop on foot patrol to let us keep the car up on the sidewalk. Some weekend days we would set up by a couple of busy bars in one of these guys' precincts and he would go into the place and send out a group of "his usual suspects" to buy chances. Sometimes they gave us the cash and didn't even bother to fill out the chance book.

The building was well maintained, but a little dated.... but the atmosphere and the ambiance was the equal of the

New York Athletic Club, the Union League or "Cheers" (which, of course, was still years away from becoming a hit TV show)

The club opened by noon each day and there were always enough retirees or guys temporarily without jobs (a big part of the membership were construction workers) to keep it financially viable. On days that he didn't go to Belmont, Aqueduct, or Yonkers to play the ponies, my grandfather, Dave Smith, could be found sitting at one of the tables in the bar with a deck of cards and a drink in front of him. Always ready for "a little game" when the younger guys started arriving in the later afternoon, the drink would usually be club soda and the game would usually be Knock Rummy. He made a living on the horses and penny-ante card games and never took enough to hurt his "customers" feelings and keep them from coming back to play regularly.

Pop, and his exploits, could almost have a chapter all his own. As a single parent, he raised a young family of five children when he lost his wife to childbirth. Later, he became unable to work as a tile-layer due to muriatic acid damage to his hands. When my mom and dad married, he moved in with them and lived off a modest disability payment... and, of course, knock rummy. He was the closest thing I ever knew to a professional gambler and would not leave our apartment without a suit and tie, a cane, and his trademark fedora. When he wasn't at the club, he frequented the local Safeway where one of the grocery clerks was also a neighborhood bookie. Since he was there so often and always so nattily dressed, newcomers to our neighborhood often approached him with shopping problems or complaints thinking he was the Safeway manager.

For years, the post was the gathering place for many of our Highbridge families and neighbors. During the week, it was the place to stop for a beer or a highball for construction workers, cops, and firemen coming home from a day of work.

When the phone behind the bar would ring, eight guys would yell in unison, "I'm not here" or "I just left."

On a Sunday afternoon after church, it became a family-oriented place where wives and family joined in and everyone was dressed in their best Sunday clothes. When the holidays came around, there was usually a Saturday night dance or a Sunday afternoon party to bring the friends together. The "Easter Parade" was usually accompanied by all of the ladies creating their own special and outlandish Easter hats replete with bunnies, chicks, and colored eggs.

As the afternoon wore on, my dad would usually sit down for an hour or two at the old upright piano and play and sing some of the popular hits of the day. Some were songs he wrote himself. Eventually, this would lead to everyone joining in to sing all their old-time favorites. I'm not sure if the picture above is an Easter Parade festivity, but all of the hats look far too sedate for it to be such.

This picture on the following page is representative of a typical Sunday afternoon at the club's bar. That's me, standing near the corner, with my father's longtime friends Artie Maddock and Herbie Doyle to my left.

Everyone of all ages just seemed to blend into one very congenial group. As I said before, it was just about the closest ambiance to "Cheers" you could think of and I will always remember it that way no matter how many years go by. Note the wall decorations… all photos of events that took place on special days at Yankee Stadium or the Polo Grounds where the Giants used to play before they moved to San Francisco. By the way, Artie was an NYPD detective and one of the ones who would take us all down to sell chances on our latest car to all his "usual suspects" in neighborhood bars and clubs in Harlem.

The Post fell on hard times once or twice and had to be closed for a few extended periods. One of these times, I remember was between World War II and Korea, but eventually, the real die-hards would find a way to make it viable again and re-open it as if nothing had ever happened. The old-timers would come flocking back to "their club" and families would resume making it the place to celebrate a family birthday, anniversary, or graduation once again. The photo on the bottom of the last page, which is from the late 1950s, is one such event that my family celebrated at the post, a christening party for my cousin Eddie Daniels.

Sadly, the day finally did come when the Edward L. Grant Post of the American Legion closed its doors for a final time. The entire character of Highbridge had changed, the Bronx was burning and those who had been the backbone of the club were moving to places like Wayne and Freehold, New Jersey and Lake Mahopac, and Huntington Station, New York. The older members of our family were seeking someplace safe and quiet to live out or begin their retirements far from the daily and nightly members, like me, were striking out to start families of our own.

The Eddie Grant Post in its heyday. If any members were around when the flag was raised or lowered, they would often come out and stand at attention for the ceremony.

I do not recall when I heard that the club had closed for the final time, but in doing some research on the internet, I learned recently that the building was an auto repair and body shop for a while. While the Post may be gone, the street outside is still called the Edward L. Grant Highway. It used to be Boscobel Avenue, named to honor a Civil War General until the members petitioned the City of New York to change it years ago. Another thing the internet brought to light and made me feel very good about was that there is now a Captain Edward L. Grant Post #75 in Franklin, Mass., which is the town where Eddie Grant was born and raised. It's nice to know that the club's identity is still out there after all this time because of all that this

Legion post meant to the hard-working, blue-collar people of Highbridge. We would seem to have reached the place where all my family and friends are fleeing the Highbridge neighborhood in which we all experienced so many new and exciting things for the very first time. We learned to be good people there and then we spread our wings and went our separate ways to start or continue families, careers, and lives that would be ever-changing as the speed of technology increased around us. I like to think, though, that anyone who grew up in a neighborhood like Highbridge in the middle of the last century will always remember it and the people they knew with a great fondness.

I loved everything about the Bronx and my Highbridge friends and neighbors and have never been reticent or shy about how I felt about the "Big Apple." It is a source of great happiness and satisfaction to me today to see how many of my children and grandchildren have come to love the city as I do even though they were mostly born and raised in New Jersey and Pennsylvania. I live vicariously through the trips they each seem to take once or twice a year and remember well the places pictured in all of their Facebook postings after each of their visits. The picture on the previous page of Ogden Avenue in the heyday of Highbridge appeared in a book by Lloyd Ultan entitled "The Beautiful Bronx 1920-1950" That's my dad in the light poplin jacket in front of the Dog and Cat Hospital and further down the avenue there's a woman in a gray coat that could be my Aunt Margaret standing out in front of the apartment house where both of our families lived for so many years. So many really good years.

The final 2 pictures show my old apartment house on Ogden Avenue as it appears today. There were no trees there when I was growing up. Herman's Store and the cleaners were on each side of the entrance to the lobby and have been replaced by two apartments (or business offices) with direct access from the sidewalk. On the second floor, right behind the tree, the far-right window (with the air conditioner) is the bedroom I shared with Pop Smith for all my school years from first grade until I graduated from Iona. Someone lives in that bedroom today and I sometimes wonder if they feel about the Highbridge of today the way I did of the Highbridge of the mid-Twentieth Century.

Dating, Courting, Marriage, & Beyond

I don't believe there could be any place in the world that would be more ideal for dating than New York City. Every kid, as they reached the dating age, was part of one of the world's largest dating pools. We were surrounded by members of the opposite sex in our apartment houses, our neighborhoods, in the schools we went to, and the dances, movies, and other forms of entertainment in which we took an active part. Our Bronx neighborhoods were "target-rich" areas to meet and date and to come of age socially.

The city had no end of places to take someone on an interesting date. There were, of course, neighborhood movie houses and school and parish dances that were great places to take a date or meet one. When you wanted to impress a girl, you had downtown movie houses, Broadway theaters, and more museums than you could visit in a dating lifetime. And not only were most of these options only a little more expensive than the local possibilities, but many of them were also free. For a couple of fifteen cent subway tokens, you could take a date to the Empire State Building, Central Park, or Times Square. Take that subway all the way to South Ferry and take a round trip ride on the Staten Island ferry for a nickel.

So there were a great many dating possibilities and plenty of places to go, but for many a guy or girl, their first encounters were hanging with the neighborhood gang on a street corner or a stoop of someone's apartment house and showing off, horsing around, flirting, giggling and appearing macho. The hoped-for end of this, at least from the guys' standpoint, would be to break off from the group and go "make out" on a bench in the local park or in an apartment house hallway. If all the stars aligned, we would take the big step to "going steady", or dating and all that other stuff above became a possibility, the museums, the zoos, the ferry, and more.

As great as the dating possibilities were in my Highbridge neighborhood in the Bronx, I seemingly went to "dating Heaven" when I became a Department of Parks lifeguard at Orchard Beach on the shores of Long Island Sound in 1952. A different girl every day was the rule of thumb for almost every lifeguard on the beach. Whether you took your lunch break with them at the cafeteria in the pavilion or joined them on their beach blanket during your breaks or asked them to go to a lifeguard beach party that night, it was all a wonderful adventure to a bunch of young teenagers with raging hormones and an unending supply of adoring young ladies. It was a whirlwind of "speed dating" before speed dating even became a thing. We discarded the ones who brought peanut butter and jelly sandwiches to share with us on a second beach visit and kept the ones who promised to bring steak sandwiches, hoagies, or cheesesteaks.

Looking back now, I still can laugh and smile at all the crazy things we did to get girls, to keep them from meeting each other, and to get to the end of the summer without getting caught. As Labor Day passed, most of us had "little black books" with enough contacts to get us through the cold months, but seldom did. Most of the summer romances were over before we lost our tans, which was usually about February when it was time to go back to the 54th Street pool in midtown Manhattan to start to get ready for the next lifeguard season.

I would be remiss in my duties as the patriarch of our family if I failed to take advantage of this "teaching moment." Over the many decades that have followed my time at the beach, I have thought often of what rotten scoundrels we were to so many young ladies for the way we treated them. When I think of how I would like my grandchildren to act, both the girls and the boys, and how I would like them to be treated, I get embarrassed a bit for the guy I once was. In my defense, I would hasten to add that I did grow and mature as those six endless summers rolled by. By my last couple of summers, some of my lifeguard buds had already met the girl they would eventually marry. I found myself just as likely to be reading or studying for the Fall semester as to still be chasing every girl who sat on a blanket on my section of the beach. It was nice, peaceful, comfortable to finally have grown up. I wound up with slightly over 500 rescues for my six years at Orchard Beach and probably close to that many dates.

On a crisp October, Sunday, my buddy Jerry and I left our neighborhood in search of some adventure, a few drinks, and a little dancing at a very popular spot at the time called the Inwood Lounge.

I was a few weeks past my final summer at Orchard Beach and the beginning of my senior year at Iona College. A couple of fairly recent graduates of Iona had started the place and it was a gold mine. The Inwood section of upper Manhattan had become the place to go for couples on a Friday night date and for singles to go on Sunday afternoons and evenings. There was a cover charge at the door, but for it, you received three tickets that were good for any drink in the house. When your tickets were gone, soda was a buck, a beer was $1.50 and a mixed drink was two dollars. It was an open secret that guys would latch onto newly arriving girls, ask them to dance and when they finally sat down would offer to go to the bar for drinks. Hopefully, the girl would offer one of her tickets to pay for her drink and ask for a Coke or Seven-Up. That was often the way it would go and the guy would go to the bar, keeping his tickets in his pocket, and pay cash for her soda and use her ticket for his beer or mixed drink. As I said, everybody knew how the game was played. Of course, a real gentleman wouldn't go off to dance with someone else when a girl's tickets ran out. But many did!

When I first saw this willowy redhead entering the lounge with her girlfriend, my mind was anywhere but on her drink tickets. As soon as was reasonably possible after they got settled, we made for their table and asked if they wanted to dance. It turned out that this beautiful Irish girl was from Washington Heights,  just across the river from Highbridge. We talked and danced the afternoon away and well into the evening and I was walking on a cloud when the Redhead and her girlfriend let me and my buddy accompany them home.

I can't count the hundreds of times I've had to listen to her tell the story of the cheap guys who took them home on the bus. That is my eternal penance for insinuating that "my wheels" were just a couple of blocks away. What can I say? I'm a guy. I didn't have much money and I didn't want her to get away.

As if that ignominious experience wasn't enough for one day, I followed up with another one just a short time later that should have ended any hope I had for a future meeting. When I was saying good night to her in her apartment house hallway. "Can I call you? Can I have your phone number, Lorraine?", I stupidly asked. (For more than sixty years, I still don't know how the name Lorraine came to my lips. I once dated a Loretta, but Lorraine continues to remain a mystery to me.) Of course, her eyes opened wide and her reply was somewhat scathing, "No. you can't have my phone number! You can't even remember my name. My name is Dorothy." Well, needless to say, a lot of groveling and desperate apologizing took place for a while. When I reached rock bottom and thought I had nothing left to bring before the court, one final argument came out for the defense. I said, "You know, you've been calling me Wes all night and I didn't say anything." Dotty looked very puzzled and said to me, "Well, isn't that your name?" I shook my head saying, "No, my name is Les." Dotty looked at me in amazement. Then she shook her head in confusion and asked, "Why didn't you say something. Why didn't you correct me?" I just shrugged my shoulders and said, "I thought you had a speech impediment." A few seconds of silence, while she stared at me, perplexed, and then broke into that fabulous laugh I would be blessed to hear the rest of my life. Our first date was over. I'd managed to snatch victory from the jaws of defeat. AND the legend of Wes and Lorraine was born. Right there, on the day we met. When we tell that story we have had our friends and family holding their sides and laughing 'til tears rolled down their cheeks and we've told it hundreds of times since that day. Needless to say, I like that story better than the "can you believe he took us home on the bus" antidote.

Dorothy Ann Adair came from good Irish stock. She was first-generation, Irish.

Her mother, Mary McGowan, came from the west of Ireland and her father, Joseph Adair, came from the north of Ireland.

I loved Molly and Joe (pictured here) from the start and

they treated me like a son from the very beginning. Our brand-new romance was full of meeting each other's relatives and friends. We both had large, extended families and our first Thanksgiving and Christmas together brought on whirlwind visits to a variety of relatives on both sides. I walked the Highbridge footbridge dozens of times to her apartment in Washington Heights. Oddly enough, although we thought of it fondly, I don't think we ever went back to the Inwood Lounge after that day we met there. We did meet at the Hi-View Tavern on 181st Street in "the Heights" at about 11:00 P.M. every Friday for the best pizza I've ever tasted. My two best friends and I had been roped into "volunteering" as bingo workers by Father Devlin, a parish Priest in my home parish of Sacred Heart Church in Highbridge.

The Bingo games at the Church were before the government got involved and put limits on how big the prizes could be in a night. Sacred Heart would get as many as 500 or more hopeful players on a Friday night and would need the auditorium, basement, and second-floor classrooms and some space in the new boys' school building to accommodate the crowd. We needed 25-30 volunteers to handle a crowd that large and that spread out. When bingo was getting close to the last game, I would call Dot and she would meet Jack, Jerry, and me at the Hi-View Tavern on 181st Street just off the Washington Bridge for a triple date with the "Bingo Boys."

We were engaged and married in less than a year and had three children before our fifth anniversary — Leslie, Matthew, and Christopher. Later on, we would be blessed with three more — Jennifer, Claudia, and Andrew. Little did I suspect, as I left my old Highbridge neighborhood in 1958, what adventures I was to have with my last and final New York date. And the "Legend of Wes and Lorraine" still continues.

Family & Personal Memories
Mom and Dad on a date to Greenwood Lake, N.J.

Me in the Bronx Home News "Most Charming Child Contest" (Honorable Mention)

Uncle Willie and me in front of Grandma's house on Sedgwick Avenue

Cousin Dave, Cousin Joan, and me in the Highbridge Park on Sedgwick Avenue under the Washington Bridge after a costume parade through the neighborhood

My sister Barbara with her doll carriage on a Sunday afternoon. (Looking north on Ogden Avenue from 170th Street)

MIAMI BOUND

My three amigos, Jerry Lenaghan, Jack Fogarty, and Tom Farrell on a trip to Coney Island. These three and I made up the "Highbridge Big Four". Friends our whole lives, Jack and Tommy and both their wives all just passed in the last five years.

131

Myself, Jerry, and Wayne Schoenwandt on the Highbridge footbridge.

Below, an enhanced 1862 photo of workmen replacing the walkway after installing a 6-foot diameter water pipe in the belly of the Highbridge "Foot- Bridge".

Grandma Fritz with me on Ogden and 168th Street on the day I made my Confirmation

A full tower at Orchard Beach with me sitting in the middle with the swagger stick. Closest to the camera is Mickey Gallagher, my partner for five summers and best friend for the rest of our lives.

The Inwood Lounge flyer I used to write down Dotty's phone number (upper right corner). This was the night we became "Wes" and "Lorraine" and the story was told for the rest of our lives.

Graduation from Iona College.

Dotty and Les, Estelle and Tom and Jerry with a date at one of my favorite "watering holes", Joe King's Rathskellar. Third Avenue and 17th Street

Coming out of church on our wedding day.

Dotty's dad, Joe Adair, and his beloved German Shepherd Watch Dog. Our kids who were born early enough to know him, loved their "Papa Joe"

I volunteered for 14 years with the Exton Little League (Exton, PA). This is a picture of coaches, managers, and umpires taken in only my first or second season with this great group of friends. I'm in the middle of the second row with the W on my ball cap. W for Wings

Our daughter, Jennifer, with her rabbit, Faith. Sadly, Jen died in an unwitnessed single-car accident on the way to her part/time job in the kitchen of a home for elderly nuns. She was 17 and about to become a high school senior

Our daughter, Claudia, graduating from High School. She would go on to become a nurse, following in the footsteps of her older sister, Leslie.

Our first child, Leslie & her husband Jerry on their wedding day. She is a Cardiac ICU nurse & they have three daughters & 3 granddaughters

Our son, Matthew, an eleven-year veteran of the Gulf War, was diagnosed with a brain tumor and passed away at age 30, leaving a wife and two daughters. Following his wishes, he was buried at sea from his third and final ship.

Claudia & Chris, High School sweethearts, married in 1991. They live in the Pittsburgh area, have three grown children. She is an E.R. supervisor.

The Turkey Point Lighthouse, just a mile and a half from our present home in North East, MD. Two of our "kids" have proposed or been proposed to at the historic lighthouse.

Our son, Christopher, and his bride, Dianne, on their wedding day in 1992. The closest to us geographically, they are a great help to us with the challenges we as octogenarians face as we gracefully age.

My old lifeguard partner, Mickey, and his wonderful wife, Rita. They were our travel companions for all our lives, but now they have both gone on without us. But I'm sure we will be meeting up again in the not too distant future

Dotty and Rita Gallagher on one of our many vacation trips together. This one to Tombstone, AZ. How fortunate can it be that two best friends meet and marry girls who become best friends, as well?

Dotty and I climbing to the top of Turkey Point Lighthouse on one of our many trips there.

The youngest of our six children, Andrew, and his lovely wife, Stacey. What else, another nurse in our family... I.C.U. They live fairly close by (in Pennsylvania) to our home on the Chesapeake Bay. They are the parents of two sons in college and two daughters in high school.

Our daughter, Leslie, in a recent picture.

Our two sons, Andy and Chris, on a recent visit.

The lovely, Miss Dotty, at the top of the lighthouse that welcomed us back for many years from cruises down the Bay.

Little Kidd Too returning to the pier after an afternoon of "tubing" with the grandchildren.

Wes and Lorraine acting up at a family get-together. Showing the younger family members how to have fun.

Sunset cruise in Saint Maarten, where we went
for seven seasons with Mick after Rita passed

Portrait with our four children at our 80th Birthday celebration. Dotty and I were born only three weeks apart. Me in Highbridge and her in Washington Heights

All set for a walk along the cliffs above the Susquehanna Flats

This lithograph hangs in my family room and always reminds me of my younger days in Highbridge and is so bitter-sweetly reminiscent of the Highbridge Big Four, Les, Jerry, Jack, and Tom. A great way and a great place to grow up.

Highbridge

The Highbridge Neighborhood today

The Bronx with an outline of the Highbridge neighborhood.

To make river traffic more navigable, three of the masonry arches of the Highbridge were removed in 1927 and replaced with a single steel span.

High Bridge, New York

An 1862 image of the 6-foot Watermain replacing the original 2 smaller pipes that were installed when the bridge was constructed between 1842 & 1847. The Highbridge was the main source of water flowing into New York City to provide fresh water from the Upstate Croton Reservoir system to the residents of Manhattan. Without the supply of freshwater New York City would never have been able to grow and prosper.

In the foreground is *The Highbridge* as it looks today.

Next in line is the Alexander Hamilton Bridge built which opened in 1963.

Furthest away is the Washington Bridge which opened in 1889. Originally built for Horse and Carriages traffic, in the early 1900s Trolly tracks were installed and the bridge was paved for automobile and bus traffic.

Ogden& University Avenues
A short walk from 1390 Ogden Avenue

Made in United States
North Haven, CT
28 March 2022

17626351R00102